T0341124

THE HEART OF LEADERSHIP

Squarely aimed at leaders and aspiring leaders, *The Heart of Leadership*, written by two renowned management experts, presents practical examples and engaging insights to answer the key question of how to be a successful leader.

This book reveals the key characteristics of a great leader and shows you how to develop the skills needed to motivate your team and overcome challenges. Leadership means successfully taking your place at the head of an enterprise and is both a shared journey and an adventure over the course of a career. Using an engaging and accessible style throughout, the book maps out how to achieve tangible results. It presents portrayals of some of history's greatest leaders, from Gandhi to Steve Jobs, from Angela Merkel to Lisa Su, in order to inspire and help develop your own top leadership skills.

This book is essential reading for CEOs, CFOs, HR managers, entrepreneurs, trainers, and those who are seeking a leadership position in an organization and want to understand how to succeed within it.

GIOVANNI BATTISTA VACCHI is currently CEO of leading furniture and design group, Colombini Group. He previously held CEO positions at Ferretti Group, Bertram Yacht, Grandi Navi Veloci, and Gruppo Zucchi, and previously worked at EY Parthenon, The Carlyle Group, and Bain & Company. He graduated cum laude from Bologna University and holds an MBA from the Tuck School at Dartmouth College.

DANILO ZATTA is a world-renowned topline growth expert and management advisor, with over 20 years' experience. He specialized in profit improvement on the revenue side, with extensive experience in strategies and leadership. He graduated cum laude from the Luiss University of Rome and holds an MBA from INSEAD and a PhD from TUM in Munich.

THE HEART OF LEADERSHIP

Giovanni Battista Vacchi and Danilo Zatta

Routledge
Taylor & Francis Group

LONDON AND NEW YORK

Designed cover image: Getty Images/ca2hill

First published 2024
by Routledge
4 Park Square, Milton Park, Abingdon, Oxon OX14 4RN

and by Routledge
605 Third Avenue, New York, NY 10158

Routledge is an imprint of the Taylor & Francis Group, an informa business

British Library Cataloguing-in-Publication Data
A catalogue record for this book is available from the British Library

Library of Congress Cataloging-in-Publication Data
Names: Vacchi, Giovanni Battista, author. | Zatta, Danilo, author.
Title: The heart of leadership / Giovanni Battista Vacchi and Danilo Zatta.
Description: Abingdon, Oxon ; New York, NY : Routledge, 2024. | Includes bibliographical references.
Identifiers: LCCN 2023044912 (print) | LCCN 2023044913 (ebook) | ISBN 9781032457475 (hardback) | ISBN 9781032463919 (paperback) | ISBN 9781003378532 (ebook)
Subjects: LCSH: Leadership. | Executive ability.
Classification: LCC HD57.7 .V33 2024 (print) | LCC HD57.7 (ebook) | DDC 658.4/092—dc23/eng/20230927
LC record available at https://lccn.loc.gov/2023044912
LC ebook record available at https://lccn.loc.gov/2023044913

ISBN: 978-1-032-45747-5 (hbk)
ISBN: 978-1-032-46391-9 (pbk)
ISBN: 978-1-003-37853-2 (ebk)

DOI: 10.4324/9781003378532

Typeset in Minion Pro
by Apex CoVantage, LLC

To my parents, Sergio and Barbara, whom I miss every day
To my wife, Benedetta, and to my children, Riccardo and Allegra,
who are my strength
To Laura
Giovanni Battista Vacchi

To my mother, Anne, and my father Renzo, whom
I always carry in my heart since their loss. To my wife,
Babette, and children, Natalie, Sebastian, and Marilena
Danilo Zatta

0 INTRODUCTION

1 ALLIANCE

2 EMPATHY

3 VISION

4 SOLITUDE & DISPENSABILITY

5

6 FOUNDATIONS

7 STATE OF LEAD

STYLE, COMMUNICATION, UNPOPULARITY, HIGHER EDUCATION

8 SELF-AWARENESS

9 DOING

10 VERTICAL HORIZON

CONTENTS

FOREWORD

In a professional context marked by complexity, changeability, and ambiguity, today's leaders have to navigate various challenges to reach their objectives, learning how to balance the arts and the sciences, and cultivating the ability to develop transversal competences, such as creativity. The World Economic Forum judges that the main challenges facing the digital age are the absence of an overall vision, the many new technologies to choose from, the presence of organizational and geographical silos, the pressure exerted by having to reach short-term results, and the lack of talent. While leaders often tend to underestimate the extent and speed of the change taking place, the ability to adapt is increasingly becoming a distinctive feature to make use of.

From reading this book, what clearly emerges is that the evolution of the model of leadership represents a priority for most contemporary organizations. Indeed, as the authors explain, teamwork, the ability to grasp opportunities (often "invisible" ones), added to the ability to establish trusting relationships between colleagues are just some of the ingredients needed to create this new leadership. The leaders who have devoted more time to managing the company, rather than to interaction, prove to be 32% less involved in their roles. In addition, for these same figures, a greater probability has been recorded (more or less twice as much) of their leaving the company within the following 12 months.

So leaders, too, are obliged to reinvent themselves and adapt to changes on the market, reaching out to identify particular and innovative ways of interacting with the various stakeholders. The awareness that the future will be marked by the words "global", "digital", "human", "competitive", and "compassionate" is growing day by day.

A theme of particular interest which emerges in much of the book is linked to the response to transformations in the environment ("Things change. And we have to change with them."). If change is constant, it is essential to have the courage to call into question traditional paradigms. With regard to remote working, Deloitte recently declared that people prove to be more productive, creative, and efficient. Moreover, a study by the Luiss Business School reveals that 75% of professionals are prepared to go on smart-working post-COVID-19, for several days a week, even consecutively.

Future leaders will increasingly be able to manage complexity, to gather and analyze the enormous amount of information available, to reach beyond their own fears, learn from their mistakes, and improve the quality of their decisions, facing the challenges of society. All this can be learned and improved on, experiencing the evolution of the organization day by day and examining the past and the present in order to build the future. The authors have chosen to use an original format in terms of both content and structure to narrate the path of the ideal leader, which combines elements of analysis and reasoning with personal, innate characteristics such as intuition.

It is precisely in the ability to range between the historical and the contemporary that this book project has its distinctive nature, succeeding in narrating entrepreneurial and managerial dynamics that can contribute to defining the salient features of the "leaders of tomorrow". The reader is guided along an authentic and detailed path of evolution in leadership, and this gives rise to important considerations and reflections.

Prof. Paolo Boccardelli
Director of the Luiss Business School

PREFACE

Leadership is "the art of getting someone else to do something you want done because he wants to do it", maintained Dwight David Eisenhower.

We also understand it as the ability to make a vision come true.

We take leadership to be **art and heart**: because good leadership must be able to get to the bottom of problems and at the same time act (not only mentally, logically, or methodically, through detailed analysis).

The leadership we have in mind is an art based on heart, passion, instinct.

As we were writing, we wondered: what sort of leadership will carry us into the future?

You're looking at a book that considers it's not just the destination that's worth the ticket but the journey, too.

We're all on board sailing towards a great adventure.

The journey towards the promised land is undertaken together, both crew and leader setting out on the route to sea, to the market.

There are many sides to a company's success: the offer of distinct products or services with a clear value, the ability to monetize the value provided to the market, innovation, and ability to adapt constantly to the way the market and customers evolve, to mention only a few of them.

One of the main factors, and the one that constitutes the *fil rouge* linking the various ingredients of corporate success, is leadership. Given that the literature generally deals with this theme from a technical and less inspirational point of view, our intention here is to make this project revolve around the criteria for a conceptual design of leadership.

To make a vision come true, several elements are needed. We have identified ten: from vision to empathy, from indispensability to doing – making it happen, from self-awareness to alliances. We have divided the book into two sections: in the first "vertical" part, it deals with themes we consider basic and structural for leadership; in the second "horizontal" part, instead, the idea is to define in a more agile and detailed fashion certain key features and passages in the way we see this vision.

To make it easier to share the experiences we have both garnered over the past decades of guiding businesses, we have decided to use the first person, though this text is the fruit of combined authorship. We emigrated as youngsters, gathering study and work experience, some on different continents. We both started working while studying. We have both guided teams of professionals. We have both started companies and both been CEOs. These parallel experiences have allowed us to acquire a shared vision.

We have also included in every chapter a mini biography of figures not necessarily connected to the business world, as examples of our way of understanding leadership.

Lastly, we should like to thank the many people who have helped us in this task. We wish to thank all those who filled the role of teachers in our lives, from parents to bosses, to the various CEOs we've had the honor to work with, to the extraordinary entrepreneurs we got to know and who inspired us, to the managers we've worked with and our co-workers on this long professional path of ours, which to date, we hope, is just one stage in a broader and more ambitious vision.

Many thanks to our closest collaborators for their critical comments and contributions to the process of the book's development: to Mauro Garofalo for his continuous and highly valuable inspiration and input and for succeeding in helping us to express our concept of leadership.

Thanks to Professor Paolo Boccardelli, Head of the Luiss Business School, who has done us the honor of writing the Preface.

Particular thanks also to Professor Luca Olivari of the Luiss Business School, as well as to Dr. Chiara Acciarini and Dr. Paola Ramirez.

We gratefully acknowledge the contribution from Andrea Sparacino and the Hoepli publishing house, who have efficiently supported the definition and realization of the editorial project.

Wishing you a good read.

Giovanni Battista Vacchi and Danilo Zatta
Bologna, Rome

Imagine all the people

DOI: 10.4324/9781003378532-1

I shut my eyes and breathe. I look around me. I take stock of all my successes, my mistakes.

What I've won, what I've lost. The people around me know.

What are the elements that have brought me here, to this precise moment? How have I changed over the years? In the end, all we can do is ask questions.

There's one thing I know, though. Or rather, I have a vision.

I know what it means to take decisions, what it means to involve people who stick alongside you and you not only esteem but, even more, they make you feel alive and happy.

Making money is not an objective. Making money is just a means of arriving at a greater aim. Bigger than me, bigger than you, even of what we call work.

There's a world behind us that forms and builds us. A geography of places that have made us what we are: imperfect beings who make mistakes.

I have always counted on my resources and those of my allies. Led battles because I believed in them, even when I was outnumbered.

I've weighed up possibilities, believing that **doing** was more important than saying. I like to be rooted in the ground, feeling the wind in my face.

I close my eyes and see myself as a man. I don't know where I am. Perhaps I'm leader of a pack. A wolf.

Whoever said that in order to be better we must draw on our human nature "only"?

The planet we live and work, travel and love on is a wonderful place: rocky crags soar in the Rocky Mountains in New Mexico, a pack of wolves roam the forests of Canada, ships sail round Cape Horn, whales spout in the Norwegian sea above the Lofoten Islands.

The animal and vegetable world, even the rocks, teach us that we are living beings in a closed system: resources are finite, and we must realize this.

As Shakespeare would say, we must bring our dreams alive: "We are such stuff as dreams are made on." And I have learned that WE CAN DO ANYTHING. We are stardust.

We live on a beautiful, interconnected planet. A pale blue dot floating in the universe, as Carl Sagan wrote in his book *Pale Blue Dot: A Vision of the Human Future in Space* commenting on the photo taken by the Voyager probe at six billion kilometers from Earth.

I see scarlet and blue skies and endless horizons. Men and women who have the role and the honor of standing at the front in the challenges that will lead us into tomorrow.

To change our times.

Make them better.

In everyday life.

The homes we live in. What we wear. How we shall move and what we shall eat. It's the little things we must be able to change. Yet how big they are.

We ourselves, before we change the world. **Together**.

Perhaps this is the biggest challenge. And we are ready.

THE LEADER IS THE PERSON AT THE HEAD OF AN ENTERPRISE

Taken both as a business company and, semantically, as action, conquest (in earlier times of a castle, today a market). Around her, or him, are the people who – in terms of affinity and ability – are in their **GROUP**. In the end we choose one another. Each with their own characteristics. Each with their own abilities. All, without exception, essential elements of the same **TEAM.**

IN THE PRESENT WE ACT OUT THE DREAM OF TOMORROW

What we decide to study, the master's degrees we do, the more or less run-of-the-mill refresher courses, our meetings with the partners at 5:00 p.m., even the squash games, the way we dress, the people we spend our lunch break with, and again the relationships we cultivate, what bank we decide will handle our finances, whether to take out a mortgage or ask for an incentive. All this, all together, is the world that makes us. Time is biunivocal, not linear.

Everything is connected.

Behind me is the person who came before me.

The perfect storm that caused me, and just me, to find myself precisely where I am (the space), in the exact moment when I am (time).

Today, tomorrow has already happened. We always move because of a vision.

Every choice I make here and now, I take because I'm thinking of an objective and want to reach it: I'm studying now to get a degree in three years' time. I'm preparing a meeting to succeed in cinching an important contract with foreign investors. I behave in a certain way – I realize what my essential bases are, what constitutes me – because I want to try and become a better person. Ten years. We only have ten years in which to demonstrate our value.

In 480 BC King Leonidas of Sparta, at Thermopylae, led just 300 Spartans into battle against the powerful Persian army. Leonidas knew he was going to die. Yet he decided to do battle against the troops of the god – King Xerxes. The Spartan had had a vision: if he gained time for reinforcements to arrive, if he managed to slow down the enemy's advance, if he managed to avoid defeat, his people would be able to go on living happily, and his wife, Gorgo (who on Leonidas's death took his place, becoming the first free woman in the West), his friends, his son . . . would live in a prosperous land: a free Greece.

This is why Leonidas decided to make his personal sacrifice. Perhaps it's a romantic idea; yet stripped of all excessive rigor, the figure of Leonidas embodies an important concept. I think the word **LEADER** might define a person who is familiar with sacrifice and the responsibility of his or her position. Whether for a narrow strip of coast or at the head of a company. A skyscraper with a thousand city lights way below it. The idea conveyed by figures such as Leonidas is filtered through elements like love, mediated by the people who are part of the team. The first amongst others, who acts with empathy and a smile on his face, understanding the difficulties of others. A Gandhi, moving the masses with the force of love, the will to win by dint of caring, without rigidity or limits.

I love my work. I love it with a vital and attentive passion. What I am trying to do here is to add narration to the gestures of a lifetime. Say the words that we use to build the world. If we understand the true name of objects, we govern them. When I say, "Let's go forward," and I do it. When I embrace someone and don't just say, "Well done." When I am at a crossroads and don't choose the road alone but take the trouble to look and see who's with me. This is the semantics of gestures. The language that takes us into the world.

Time is not linear.
Everything is interconnected.
Behind me is everything that came before me. The *perfect storm* that caused me, and just me, to find myself precisely where I am, what I am in.
Today happens because it has already happened tomorrow.
The force of vision is what counts.

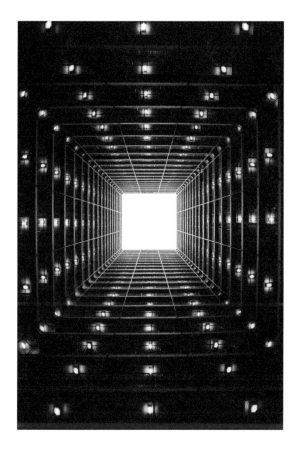

BEING THE FATHER OF YOUR OWN STORY

Every father leads you by the hand. Being a father means understanding that we are unique, individual beings.

According to the Treccani dictionary, *educe˘ re* (i.e., "draw out", "pull out", or "draw out what is inside") derives from the combination of *e* – ("from, out of") and *duce˘ re* ("to lead"). What is to be understood is "in particular, the process of cultural transmission, which differs according to each historical and culturally determined situation, through which, within determined social institutions (family, school etc.), the human personality is structured and integrated into society".

My father was always present: he was a successful freelance professional, the child of that middle class that over the centuries has been a bearer of revolutions. Like everyone, he experienced success and failure, but he never hesitated to offer praise for what I was doing. He was the one who taught me the importance of words. The attitude of positive reinforcement instead of severity. I can still see his ambitions for my results. Yet he was a man who never asked. He was just happy for my successes. He never wanted anything for himself. Nothing was owed. On the contrary, he taught me to question the intention of things.

How much are you prepared to *sacrifice* to achieve your result? How much are you prepared *to lose?*

PHILOSOPHICAL QUESTIONS

He let me pursue my desires and my passions, whether it was a matter of studies, profession, or sport. He secretly delighted in my successes. I could even hear what he didn't say to me but what he somehow allowed me to understand. The weight of those non-words deposited inside me in the form of security. If, today, I am convinced, as far as possible, of what I do and of the choices I've made, I owe it to this man who was happy about what his son was deciding to be and to become. I found out from my mother and from his friends how proud he'd been of the boy I was. He died when I was 23 and he was 58. He had always worked for his family and his parents.

I remember a good man. Who handed down to me values to which I then attached other words: **AMBITION** for professional success, **DETERMINATION, DEVOTION, LUCK, SACRIFICE, COMPREHENSION, GOOD CHEER**. He was someone who found a positive side to things even in the midst of difficulties. And even in dark times he made himself leave his problems aside, not letting them show through and managing to be a barycenter for all those he loved.

Compared to him, I'm still a father who hugs, but stricter and more ambitious, above all in terms of my children's choices and objectives. I vigorously try to instill a work ethic in them; at the same time I find myself more pedantic in demanding effort and sacrifice. I do it for their own happiness, not asking them to be like me but insisting that they do their best on the path they choose to follow. And I ask the same of my co-workers.

It's an attitude that must always accompany someone who has to take decisions. Exploiting the talents one has and being ambitious in developing and strengthening them. Basically **a GIFT**, a talent, must never be wasted. Commitment, hard sweat, and sacrifice are needed.

Choose here and now.

As far as I'm concerned, I try to obtain the "best" through love, a smile, and motivation. The vehicles of success I'm working on now all focus on creating a strong team. We live in a complex world that moves quickly. I measure a team's strength in terms of its cohesion. **A CHAIN IS AS STRONG AS ITS WEAKEST LINK**: I very much appreciate these words from the book *One Life* (1969) by Christian Neethling Barnard, the world-famous South African surgeon who performed the world's first heart transplant.

An enterprise can be seen as a beating heart. **THE DESIRE FOR ENTREPRENEURSHIP** belongs to those with an objective and a direction. The people who make up the expedition are the heartbeat and breath of the adventure. Only when heart and mind work in harmony is an organism able to give its best. It is then that time deconstructs, and there is the onset of what in sport is defined as the state of flow, that is, the perfect moment when you enter an agonistic trance: time deconstructs, and everything seems to last longer. But this is only because you are so concentrated that you can see every single instant. To get to this level, though, you have to have repeated the gesture endless times. To be there, you have to have **TRAINED RIGOROUSLY FOR YEARS**. Repeating the movement until it's been perfected. Until the rhythm has been assimilated. At this point, you can overcome any obstacle – time "lasts" longer.

My objective is that in my chain – my team – there are no weak links and, if instead there should be, they are reinforced and protected.

What If: The Future
In the tomorrow I have in mind an even more global world exists. We get to tomorrow with
STRONG PEOPLE INTERNATIONALIZATION GLOBAL PRESENCE

USE OF TECHNOLOGY THE WORLD OF AI (ARTIFICIAL INTELLIGENCE)

With tools that lead us into the future, data on the products chosen by the customers of the future, buying habits discovered:

- on the social networks;
- on the web;
- by constant listening and interaction, using every touchpoint available with our customers.

BIG DATA ARE PRODROMAL TO THE DEVELOPMENT OF INNOVATIVE SERVICES

You get to the *Land of Tomorrow* by using the attitude of Iron Man, a scientist who uses technology for the greater good. Like the Space X project of Elon Musk, who, after inventing Tesla, travels to Mars, or like Jeff Bezos' Amazon, when he built a marketplace for selling online 25 years ago. You get there in the spirit of the innovator who shoulders the risks of being considered "too far in advance", a visionary.

"Limits are made to be overcome." *Tony Stark*

THE FUTURE IS A GREAT FOREST TO BE TRAVELLED THROUGH

We know that inside it we shall come across numerous obstacles and dangers that can make us change to a new path at any time. Yet it is precisely by facing them that we strengthen our determination. And by facing the fear that defeats the fear of being afraid. At the same time the path before us will reveal itself.

If the dangers can be identified, they can also be fought, and you will even be able to change direction. At the end of the forest there is light, the sun. The knot will unravel and then, if you like, you will be able to go on and walk through another stretch of forest. The future is a constant journey as the world goes forward. It's a suspended place with dangerous animals and chasms, trees and branches to be cut through, rivers, rapids, and waterfalls. Yet if you think about it, a waterfall never "falls". And we know for certain that sooner or later the world has to be faced up to.

PART I

Vertical

Future, birth, and psychology of a leader

CHAPTER 1
Alliance

DOI: 10.4324/9781003378532-3

When – in one of the best-known and most fascinating stories in Greek mythology – Jason sets out on his search for the Golden Fleece, he chooses the best men to sail out on the Argus towards the land of Colchis: among the 50 heroes, the Argonauts, we find Hercules with his superhuman strength; the *Dioscuri* – Castor and Pollux, the Spartan warrior brothers; Orpheus. who could tame wild beasts; Theseus, who succeeded in escaping from the Minotaur's labyrinth.

The word **LEADERSHIP** can be taken apart: there's the noun, **LEADER**, with the suffix of Navigation – **SHIP**. And in this way the meaning of leadership assumes the connotations of a voyage understood as a collective project with the crew as an extension of alliance – the 50 heroes, the Argonauts – the winning team. A leader can be recognized in the alliances they are able to form, the gentlemen's agreement sealed with a handshake, well before the due contractual formalities.

Or better, they can be recognized by the **AUTHORITY** with which they are able to engage those who most deserve it. This is why the "true" leader boards the vessel with the best of them.

The crew will want to set out, because the adventure is worth it and because they feel the aim of the voyage is their own. They were intrigued from the very first moment they were taken on board. Because the leader is a visionary, a storyteller.

A true leader is able to conjure up dreams before enterprises and to instill confidence in the result.

They show us lands we didn't even know about, the future that will be – the Golden Fleece – the dream not of mere riches, so much as of success, the glorious enterprise.

Because the leader is an evocation in themselves, the captain, and at the same time, the vessel.

But they know that for the enterprise, they need to be surrounded by people who are better than them. *You must be capable of attracting the giants.*

The leader themselves is an evocation, the captain, and at the same time the vessel, the vision, and the route.

The Qualities of Being/Having

You might be asked to found a branch of a multinational. Working in Italy, the United States, Germany, **anywhere in the world**, you will always have a series of problems: access to a customer network; knowledge of the market in question; identifying important objectives regarding growth and turnover; time (wretched time, which is always lacking – **À LA RECHERCHE** – the time we don't have, and which therefore mustn't be wasted, or time scrunched up – **DU TEMPS PERDU** – and thrown away!).

Such important tasks can only be dealt with by forming competent teams, an attack by giants (as in the popular Japanese manga and anime series our children watch): people with solid qualifications and an impeccable track record, each of whom is the best in their field.

Numbers, words, mathematics, physics, engineering, it's all music, all an amalgam, transversal competences to be declined, put in line, oriented, pointed in the right direction – anything can be declined (in as many ways you can imagine).

The leader is capable of bringing together competences; this is why they're the conductor of the orchestra.

I find the best people are the ones who come to you and say, "Don't fret, I'll take care of it", plunging right in and treating business problems as if solving them were their personal objective – the path to travel and the route their own.

And basically, if you think about it, that's just how it is.

If you're on board a ship in the middle of the ocean, what happens to the vessel, to the other crew members, happens to you too.

Choices are **stretches** of that intricate forest, which we call days.

Every day brings you closer to the next stretch.

Whether you take that train or you don't take it, these are already two different futures.

Every act you perform – swabbing the bridge, plotting the route, keeping a lookout on the limit marking the horizon between sea and sky – represents another league covered on the map, an extra knot on your cruising speed.

In the specific story represented by every company, the leader must choose what direction to take, the geography, and the embarkation are the mathematics of the voyage.

The path the leader takes is the primary narrative crossroads before all that comes later.

I get rid of a branch of the company and improve the conditions of the whole group.
Or
I keep it and let the ship sink.

TO TAKE IMPORTANT DECISIONS, THE LEADER HAS TO BE ABLE TO TRUST THEIR CREW

As for the Argonauts, if the leader has taken only the best on board, what they choose will be the synthesis of all they see, hear, and shape according to their vision. Every element of the expedition controls a single piece of the collective voyage. And the leader knows that to succeed in the enterprise, they must be able to trust every person in the team. The necessary and sufficient elements for a concept of enterprise are those that give everything in order to reach the objectives. Their vision and spirit of sacrifice are what makes the crew essential to the voyage. A ship doesn't exist without a captain, but at the same time it's made of wood and sailors, hold and ropes, a route, full sails.

THOSE WHO ARE INDISPENSABLE ON BOARD ARE THOSE WHO BRING THEIR WILL TO "DO" AND MAKE THE ENTERPRISE HAPPEN

I don't consider people who guide a team arrogantly to be indispensable; this is an attitude that risks underestimating things, ploughing ahead, and not seeing the danger hidden in the depths of the seas and the forests; behavior like this results, in the best of hypotheses, in the failure of the expedition.

THE HEROES WHO CARRY OUT THE ENTERPRISE ARE ALL THOSE WHO HAVE A VISION AND SHARE IT WITH YOU WITHOUT EVER BEING ENSLAVED, but staying on the lookout for danger, even when you don't notice it, those who think and speak out. They think for themselves, and that's why they're all the more precious. Just passing clouds in the wind. Breathe, they tell you. Breathe the breath of the world. So vast and wonderful.

In all my experiences there has been a co-worker who, for one reason or another, has changed roles and yet remained somehow a precious resource. Those who from being simple co-workers, have started to work on strategic growth projects. Those who have had to move because of reorganization. I admire those who put aside their past experiences and see them for what they are. A basis for the next stage of evolution. A useful cluster for building competences.

To the same extent, those who have a passion for a new job and see it as a further stage in drawing closer to a common objective are essential to the success of an enterprise. And for this reason they behave with awareness and the ability to look at the stretch of coast they are navigating – here and now – always succeeding in seeing what must be done to disentangle themselves, if necessary being capable of finding a solution, inventing one or demanding one from internal or external resources, as required.

WHAT IS IMPORTANT IS TO MOVE FORWARD – IT IS THE VISION

If we have used all our knowledge, even if we lose in the end, in a sense we have won all the same. When I was working at Zucchi Bassetti on restructuring the company – an extremely complex process but one that contributed to recovering the company's health and saving it – a young colleague helped me to find my way through the tangles of a situation that had become chronic and another senior co-worker made himself totally available to the new boss, filling me in on the mechanisms he had learned over years of experience.

This is how we succeed, by sharing our path, our knowledge and placing it all at the service of the project. Nature is collaborative. In the same way, human beings must cooperate. To the utmost of our capacity.

"Nature is the source of all knowledge. She has her own logic, her own laws, no effect without cause, or invention without necessity."
Leonardo da Vinci

It is absolutely essential to collaborate; we must all compete against the enemy. Enemies are our competitors but also the market, which ought to be a friend since it is the habitat of any company.

The enemy should not be seen just as an adversary, negative – an evil. This would be an oversimplification. Our real enemy is the comparison, and we know that we ourselves are really the enemy. Outside are the challenges of the world in which we shall have to be competitive.

Where the market appears with its ruthless laws of efficiency and productivity, demand and offer, where there are delicate moments and epic crises, external factors, and we have to decide whether to accept defeat or be Spartan and send back Xerxes' messengers, who demand that we bow down to their rules.

Look around us and acknowledge what it's worth for us.

The wheat fields where the bread that arrives on our tables is grown, the walls of the city we live in – that **unique** place that we call "home" – our children running along the beach in summer, their friends, their first loves.

The people who've supported us, breathing in the air of the world we ourselves have contributed to forming.

Because it's nature and human beings that form things, and this form bears within it the substance of what they will become.

It's no coincidence that the word **rival** (taken here as a competitor) comes from the Latin *rivalis*, that is, the one who shares the water in the river with another person in order to irrigate his own field: the word *rivalis* derives from *rivus*, river or stream.

Rivals are whoever find themselves in the same position as us of having to access limited sources.

So the solution is not always a strong arm and the extermination of the other. The point is to grasp the concept of water. Sometimes the stream swells with rain. Overflowing, the water sweeps with it everything on its path.

FROM WATER WE MUST LEARN TO BECOME A TEAM THAT WINS COMPLICATED BATTLES

When we have to win market shares, for example, we must be animated by a competitive spirit that guides us along our path where, when it's a matter of the course of events, it's always foreseen that someone will win, and consequently, someone else will lose.

Before every match, the powerful New Zealanders in the All Blacks rugby team roar their **HAKA** against the enemy. A dance that incorporates terror and invocation but also an homage to the strength of our adversaries, whose valor we are even grateful for, because without it we wouldn't be engaging battle, and so what would remain of us? Desires and air. Like this, the players annihilate competitors with their show of strength. In reality they're preparing for the outcome of the battle. For the demons that might, on a whim or out of necessity, make them lose the game. If I win, I accept that someone will lose.

That someone might even be me.

So how much am I prepared to risk? And above all, am I capable of carrying the weight, accepting my destiny, even that of a possible defeat?

WHEN I COMPETE, I OBVIOUSLY DO SO IN ORDER TO WIN, YET THE WATER FLOWS ON, AND I CANNOT TAKE ANYTHING FOR GRANTED

A team is as strong as its weakest player.

Within a company everything revolves around the concept of the chain, of link following link or, as an alternative, of the pack. A team is as strong as its weakest player.

This is why we should make one another stronger, work together, even challenge one another internally, not so much competitively as to work towards mutual improvement.

If I know that my companion in the enterprise is giving 110%, I won't want to contribute a mere 50. This is the stimulus of reinforcement.

This is why everyone needs to cooperate, to push themselves towards the best they can give. To the enterprise, true, but deep down for themselves.

In this sense leadership means knowing when certain people have no intention of tackling the forest alongside you. Perhaps it's of no interest to them. Or they have reasons connected to specific inhibitions.

Facing the dangers of the forest, setting out on an unknown route with someone who isn't going to watch your back or be capable of judging the distance from the land to the horizon becomes extremely wearing.

IN NATURE, THE HEAD OF THE PACK DECIDES WHO SHOULD BE REPLACED IN THE GROUP IT ISN'T AN EASY DECISION AT ALL, BUT NECESSARY FOR THE WHOLE PACK TO BE ABLE TO MOVE FORWARD

The company is an orchestra. Half classical, where everything must work with a rhythm and a direction, and each player has his own part of the score, but the music of a company is also the Rolling Stones, rock, vision. The great idea that, yes, it's even possible to change paradigms. By your own example. Which will last even after we have disappeared.

THE LEADER IS SIMPLY A *PRIMUS INTER PARES* AMONGST STRONG PEOPLE, WHERE EVERYONE PLAYS THEIR OWN ROLE AND TRIES TO BE THE BEST THEY CAN

This characterizes and defines a successful company.

When you're a woman, many people think you're worth less. Not so much in terms of ability, as in reliability and "grip". They think you'll probably act less vigorously compared to a man. That you won't be able to shake as many hands. You'll make less money.

Alliance | Angela Merkel
Politician

When you're a woman, many people think you're worth less. Not so much in terms of ability, as in reliability and "grip". They think you'll probably act less vigorously compared to a man. That you won't be able to shake as many hands. You'll make less money. This means you'll be worth less on the market, you'll earn less, and you'll be less respected. Legs before brain. And instead.

When she was born in Hamburg in 1954, it was already quite clear that Angela Merkel's path would cross that of the world's leading figures, she'd be a leader capable of banging a fist on the table and, at the same time, keeping alive the unbiased force of passion: her father was a Lutheran pastor, and from him she probably inherited discipline and her love of studying. Her mother was a teacher of Latin and English. Her grandparents lived in East Prussia – the geography of a **WORLD BELONGING TO YESTERDAY**, when men had moustaches and girls wore tulle dresses and full skirts, elegant beneath the chandeliers of the Ballhaus.

As she grew up, Angela learned Russian, became a member of the German young Socialists movement, and went on to get a degree in quantum chemistry.

After the fall of the Berlin Wall in 1989 and the free elections of March 1990, she became spokesperson of the GDR's last government before East and West Germany were reunited.

After her election as a member of the Bundestag – the German Parliament – in December of the same year she was appointed secretary-general of the CDU. Finally she was elected by a center-right coalition, the Große Koalition, and in 2005 sworn in as chancellor before the German people. Angela Merkel stands out for her firm positions and at the same time is gifted with a clear vision, which does not always meet with acclaim from everyone.

Popularity is not one of her main objectives; indeed she appears rather as a leader of **ALLIANCES**: the first thing she did after being elected to her first term of office was visit the then prime minister of France, Jacques Chirac, to consolidate the French-German axis within the European Union. Merkel also takes risks, as well as "difficult" decisions, as when she visited the Dalai Lama Tenzin Gyatso in 2007, a decision that made diplomatic relations between Germany and China considerably cooler. By the time she had reached her fourth consecutive term of office in 2018, Merkel was often compared to England's "Iron Lady", Margaret Thatcher, due particularly to her conservative positions (as in the case of her "no" to gay marriage in 2017, although she left the MPs in her own party complete freedom to vote). She was the first elected chancellor to come from former East Germany.

A curiosity: her maiden name is Kasner, and the surname she is known by to the whole world is actually that of her first husband, then a physics student, Ulrich Merkel. At present she is remarried to the German chemist and physicist Joachim Sauer. According to *Forbes* magazine, Angela Merkel comes top in the classification of the world's most powerful women.

KEY TAKEAWAYS

"Our" leader

- always has a vision;
- is capable of attracting giants (the best in each sector);
- has confidence in their team (the orchestra);
- is capable of team building, strengthening (or replacing) their weakest player;
- has authority;
- is capable of cooperating;
- is a *primus inter pares.*

Every day brings with it millions of invisible opportunities

CHAPTER 2

Empathy

DOI: 10.4324/9781003378532-4

Dawn.

The gleam of a dewdrop in the light.

A leaf leans towards morning. And unfurls. A movement unseen and barely perceptible. Yet it happens.

Every day brings with it millions of invisible opportunities. How open are we to welcoming these opportunities?

How much practice will it take?

Even the way we breathe makes a difference, the short breaths that bring an immediate result or instead the air that slowly swells our lungs and chest, with blood filling the rib cage, the solar plexus, and from there the shoulders, the forearms, the hands.

These hands that grip other hands, pick up the pen, figure out elaborate strategies and the bold ascent to success.

Our lifestyle, the one we believe in, talent, the way we stir the sugar into our coffee or offer it to guests, perfection in every gesture.

A leader knows how important it is to be a motivating factor for their co-workers.

A leader manages to create a relationship with their co-workers that extends beyond working life.

THE LEADER CAN LAUGH ALONG WITH THE TEAM
THE LEADER ACKNOWLEDGES VALUE
AT THE SAME TIME, A LEADER KNOWS WHEN IT'S
TIME TO PLAY TOUGH

Time for the trial of strength. And then they **ENGAGE** and accept the challenge. Expects the best from everyone. Even taking on board the mistakes – which they must take on board – and the responsibility for them. A "real" leader knows when to take decisions and what moves to make on the chessboard. And when things have gone well, there, too, the leader distinguishes themselves, because they can let go. Release the moorings. The control. Cast off and untie the knots because they've led into **STRAITS**. And straits, unlike knots, which fasten and block, are passages that compel agnition. When you've navigated them, you have acquired greater knowledge and ability.

It really is a matter of leader-ship.

A leader knows they can't obtain the utmost if a relationship is purely mental or rational.

TO OBTAIN THE UTMOST, THE UTMOST IS NEEDED: head, brain, and above all, heart. If just one of these jewels is missing, the evocation will not be complete. The void that ensues will cloud all vision. Instead, a leader is able to move people according to how they narrate the story: more than what they say, it will be their empathy, the mood created, that makes the difference.

We are not persuaded to do something or not do it for rational reasons alone: there's an element of intuition, linked to the story that the idea inspires in us. And it's this pregnancy that will lead us to follow that particular captain onto that particular ship.

A leader knows that to obtain the utmost, the utmost is needed. Head, brain, and heart.

Some people have this vision according to which part of life is devoted to work and the other is personal. Today I think most people spend a good deal more time at work than they do with their loved ones. This isn't the "best" scenario. It's a fact. A quantitative observation, which certainly doesn't say anything about the quality of the time shared. Or rather, it's true for all those who have jobs they like and in which they are successful in different ways.

To me an empathetic attitude means managing to establish trusting relationships with others. Those who work with you (and the difference can be seen here: in the use of the preposition "with" instead of simply "for", implying a linear, inclusive, collaborative, and non-subordinate relationship with co-workers) must know that they can count on a "friend". Someone who understands them. Who assigns them functions but at the same time acknowledges their depth and their needs, **FROM ONE HUMAN BEING TO ANOTHER**.

This should never be forgotten. It doesn't mean that performance is not demanded or results not expected. But I believe that when a person needs an exchange, it is essential for them not to feel intimidated. Every time you have an opinion or when, during brainstorming with the boss, you don't agree, your impetus is of basic importance, just as listening is: if we don't understand something, this may depend on our not being capable of it, of our understanding being limited by incomplete information or on our being victims of prejudices we aren't aware of. Here, on the other hand, we have an open and honest exchange and an opportunity for growth. For all the people involved in the decision-making process. This is the only way we can get through the forest. Together.

PERHAPS YOU YOURSELF HAVEN'T NOTICED THE POTHOLE ON THE PATH, AND INSTEAD SOMEONE ELSE HAS NOTICED IT FOR YOU

If when negotiating the minefield of existence, things should go well this time, we shall all move forward. Whilst waiting to see what awaits us. Tomorrow.

We are all individuals.

We all come from our own path. And then we find ourselves facing trials and whole days together, the harsh sound made by "Time, the great sculptor", as Marguerite Yourcenar, the French writer and poetess and first woman elected to the Académie Française, defines it: "Everything flows. The soul, watching in stillness the passage of joys, sadness and deaths, which life is made up of, has received the 'great lessons of things passing.'"

We are all Spartans on the road to Thermopylae. Our shields on our right arm, spears in hand, we march on tirelessly. Without fear, we march on. And even if there were gods before us, let the heavens and the thunderbolts rain down upon us!

When we work together, facing the sea and the tides, we all tackle the fluctuations of the market, work, the economic crises, and it's then that we must remember the dignity of those who came before us, like the pictures of the men and women on the poster for the 1978 film *F.I.S.T.* directed by Norman Jewison. A story of working men and women like us, with the trade unions following Sylvester Stallone: "A love story between a man, a Country, the people he led and the woman he loved."

SHARING EMOTIONS BECAUSE ENTERPRISE COMES FROM THE HEART BEFORE ALL THE REST

The great advantage held by CEOs, leaders, heads of companies who work in close contact with their co-workers is that some people are immersed in day-to-day work – the tangled forest of the daily tasks that demand immediate solutions. And they risk missing the general overview, trapped as they are in the undergrowth because perhaps they haven't paid enough attention to the narrow way out, which would allow them to escape a certain situation quite easily. This, then, is the importance of being part of a strong and devoted team that can clearly see the landmarks along the way. The ways out to success.

In all this the leader has the advantage of looking down from above, detached and drawing scale benefits from other peoples' *Weltanschauung* and assumes the burden of decisions, imagining the possibilities, and weighing up the best solution to take, on the basis of the different routes proposed. In some ways the leader might be compared to a peregrine falcon, though less aggressive. I like to think of a leader as a man or woman on top of a mountain. Thinking from those dizzy heights. Beneath their eyes the glorious red of living earth on the horizon, the green woods of dense vegetation, the Rocky Mountains all around and in front the endless sky of the United States.

THE COLOR OF LEADERSHIP IS BLUE BECAUSE THE TRANSPARENT BLUE SKY MAKES VISION POSSIBLE

It carries you off into splendid, uncontaminated worlds: the North Pole which is considered pure white. Blue is the color of the sky and at the same time of the sea. The border between the heights and the depths. And we are tightrope walkers on the narrow line of existence. It's the blue that makes the Sun so radiant.

It's a color synonymous with excellence, often chosen to represent chromatically a big company's top-quality products; it conjures up the concept of **WELL MADE**, of **BEAUTY** and what human beings are capable of producing, the magnificence of the work of art that accompanies our history. The culture and knowledge of humankind on the planet Earth.

"It's actions that count. Our thoughts, however good they may be, are fake pearls until they're transformed into actions. Be the change you want to see in the world."

Empathy | Gandhi
Father of the nation

A breath of wind and then. Waking up in the morning. Hands against the earth, wood, bare feet, the cotton khadi brushing the ground. Outside, birds are waking up the world. And you, eyes closed, try to feel your breathing. What connects you to Everything, of which we are all a part.

Gandhi, mahatma, the "great soul", was the leader of India's independence, its nonviolent revolution based on *satyagraha*, a word made up of the two Sanskrit words *satya*, "truth", and *ahimsa*, "nonviolence", "love".

Gandhi was the leader of mass civil disobedience, the peaceful strength of right. A master who made the philosophy of the rock the voice of an entire people.

"It's actions that count. Our thoughts, good though they may be, are fake pearls until they are transformed into actions. Be the change you want to see in the world."

Empathetic, solid, capable of conveying the "goodness" and "rightness" of his positions to an enormous audience through his effective *ars oratoria* based on peacefulness: his voice, the sound of a stream running and the vitality of grass growing, the good humor of the oxen drawing the plough, the dignity of men's and women's work in the fields, the sweat and labour of endless days.

Born in 1869, son of a well-to-do Hindu – the surname Gandhi means "grocer", tradesman – at 13 he made an arranged marriage, as was then the custom, to a girl the same age (what he would later define as "the cruel custom of child marriages"); at 18 he moved to study law in England, where it was impossible for him to follow religious practices and he was therefore declared a *paria*, or "casteless".

When he got back to his homeland he discovered that, following the death of his father, his beloved mother had also died.

How do you explain a blade of grass?

Barefoot, after the Salt March and the First and Second World Wars, the Quit India movement encouraged total, nonviolent rebellion as desired by the Mahatma; great protest marches were organized, of such import that the United Kingdom, giving in to the pressures of the anti-colonial movement, finally granted full independence.

Gandhi was the prime example of leadership based on humility. He led a sober life, devoting care and attention to the weakest of people. When he was assassinated in January 1948, the Indian Prime Minister Jawaharlal Nehru, one of the foremost political figures in the world, commenting on Gandhi's death on the radio, said as follows:

> Friends and comrades, the light has gone out of our lives, there is darkness everywhere and I do not know what to tell you or how to tell it. Our beloved leader *Bapu*, as we called him, the father of the nation, is no more. Perhaps I am wrong to say that. Nevertheless,

we shall no longer see him as we have seen him all these many years, we shall no longer run to him for advice or seek solace from him and that is a terrible blow, not to me only but to millions and millions of people in this country.

KEY TAKEAWAYS

"Our" leader

- understands everyday opportunities;
- can motivate people and acknowledge value;
- knows that to obtain the utmost, the utmost is needed;
- travels through the forest together;
- appreciates transparency, like the blue of the sky;
- establishes a trusting relationship with others.

CHAPTER 3
Vision

DOI: 10.4324/9781003378532-5

The ability to look ahead and further.

VISION for a leader means half the job is already done. I use my eyes to look. Colors, shapes, an intense glare. How many mirages have we come across on our way here? Just think of stolen love, lost love, falling in love with a woman or a man, an idea – how much did we believe in all these?

WHAT MUSIC WERE YOU LISTENING TO WHILE YOUR WORLD, AS YOU KNEW IT, COLLAPSED AROUND YOU? AND THEN, BEFORE YOUR VERY DISILLUSIONED EYES, MAGICALLY RECOMPOSED ITSELF?

A new job. A new opportunity. A new love. The unexpected turn of events.

INTUITION means having a gut feeling for solving complex problems. Without your thoughts getting tangled up and going round in circles, which would only bring all strategic thinking back to square one. As though in a labyrinth. And here Calvino and Jorge Luis Borges were right. In the "labyrinth of the contemporary condition" there is no longer a Minotaur. The great challenge for today's men and women is more complex than the one faced by the ancient Greeks. Today *we are* the labyrinth.

Intuition is innate. It's the *quid*.

Something you have and think you should listen to, persistently.

WE HAVE TO ACCEPT THAT INTUITION IS PART OF US

I'm not talking here about animal instinct but what, in some managerial logics, is defined "hypothesis first". You start out from a concept, a vision coming from the gut but approved by quantitative data analyses, sharing strategic thinking with your team. Only then is that intuition translated into an idea to be pursued.

INTUITION IS FOLLOWED UP BY THE REAL MANAGERIAL WORK, WHICH HAS TO PROVE THAT THE HYPOTHESIS IS ON THE RIGHT TRACK

This is done through a series of bridges, links, possible developments, sub-hypotheses, axioms including set analyses. All that is defined in consultancy as proto-managerial work and choice support – the item defined by the acronym MECE, Mutually Exclusive Collectively Exhaustive – a grid of links and conjectures, each of which proves the concept expressed by the previous hypothesis. This is one of the concepts of analysis used as a basis by big companies, such as Bain & Company, McKinsey & Company, and many managers from the leading schools.

HAVING AN INTUITION IS LIKE SEEING A COMET

Glimpsing a sparkle in the sky and knowing that you've seen it, yet its shining trail will not endure. It isn't absolute. Perhaps nothing is. First you must grasp the intuition and stare hard at it, then you'll be able to find it amongst a million **STARS** in the night. All you know is that you have seen it.

The idea conveyed by the intuition is there: but "there" where? And is it real or not?

This is why **a leader's intuition has to do with their dream**. The world imagined by Steve Jobs, the vision of Apple, which is not "just" the apple but rather a mindset, a way of behaving, dressing, "dressing" your ideas.

AND WHO, BEFORE STEVE JOBS, WOULD EVER HAVE SAID THAT THIS VISION GENERATED IN A LITTLE BACKROOM BY A GROUP OF NERDS WOULD ONE DAY NOT ONLY EXPLODE BUT EVEN, IN ITS OWN WAY, CONQUER THE WORLD?

Things change. And we have to change with them.

It is frequently intuition that guides us. When you re-structure a company that has a majority share in another, many people might think of the other company as a hidden "treasure" belonging to the head of the group. And then along you come and have the intuition that it's something quite different: something to get rid of immediately.

So there's a company we shall call X. At that particular moment the company is underperforming and holds majority shares in another company we shall call Y, one that in the past was an authentic warhorse. But what about today? That's what you must always ask yourself.

In fact Y produces only one type of goods: a way of working that has been a winner up to now. And we all know, when things work well, how does the saying go? "Don't change a winning team", "If it ain't broke, don't fix it." And yet . . .

There's this thing called intuition that tells you that, instead of thinking about what product to offer customers on the basis of what they desire – and desires grow, change, and everything changes – the mother company is obliging itself to buy everything factory Y produces, because of that past relationship (the weight of heritage). And instead, have you ever asked yourself what alternative sources of supply you have, for example?

ON A QUICKLY CHANGING MARKET, YOU HAVE TO DIFFERENTIATE

Things change. And we have to change with them.

DESTRUCTURING is therefore the only path that will allow you to see things as they really are, not as you want them to be, or what they were. Destructuring, getting rid of the structures, all that weighs you down, seeing what's there, spurious, linear, in its pure, unadulterated, and magnificent essentiality.

Is time a circular or linear variable?

Time is linear.

It's a vision, from here and now to the future.

A straight line leading towards an ambition.

A straight line that runs right to the end of that ambition, then starts out again from there and rethinks itself.

A route.

And you know the direction of that path, but you don't know if there are roadworks en route, or whether you may be obliged to take a deviation. The important thing is to get to the end of the journey, the objective of your route.

There may be waystages:

To be ambitious, a long-term line must estimate that accomplishing the vision will take at least ten years.

Achieving a good halfway stage instead will take about five with shorter intervals that may last from one to two years.

In an overall vision you must be able to climb mountains, know the best road back or the one to travel if obstacles crop up. You must time the waystages – or reflect on the milestones to be paused at – and even estimate the energy it will take for the return journey. Vision in a complex, long-term project takes the same work as is necessary for building a house. Before the walls are raised, the foundations have to be put down and the power circuits provided for, before laying the floors, adding the finishing touches, furnishing and putting up pictures.

THE FUTURE, TOMORROW, HAS AN IMPACT ON TODAY

I have the utmost respect for yesterday.

I DETERMINE MY TODAY BY LOOKING TO THE FUTURE

I study the past, what has been, and on reflection it was none other than a series of todays at the moment when they were conceived, todays looking to the future – to our present. This, then, is the explanation for the correlation between events so far distant from one another. For the way one choice impacts on those to come and, on the contrary, for what we have today and owe, for better or for worse, to situations that occurred at a time before us. So we should always ask ourselves if the choices we inherit are the right ones for today or, better, if they were "right" for the moment when they were taken but now it might be as well to intervene and change them. We must always look to the future whilst respecting the past. To me this means that when you are in the midst of a process of change, such as the restructuring of a company, for example – or even when we're not talking about the growth of a complex organism like a company but about individual growth – the past should be appreciated, in the sense that radical change is per se a potential element of risk.

ONE OF THE ESSENTIAL VEHICLES, CHANGE AND INNOVATION, MUST ALWAYS BE TAKEN ADVANTAGE OF, BEARING IN MIND THE MACROCOSMOS WE ARE PART OF

If I enter a corporation, the first thing to do, for example, is to make a distinction between companies that are doing well and those that are not. If they're not doing well, then I shall necessarily have to make changes, so as to lead them back to recovery. Instead, we have to maintain the success of the ones that are doing well. In the former case, a greater change will probably be necessary than in the latter.

If you're a doctor and examine a patient in good health, you'll go carefully, perhaps try to improve his physical shape, maybe put him on a diet or prescribe physical exercise, and this will bring a shot of lymph within a general condition of well-being: and a doctor knows how to offer treatment without turning things upside down. A leader follows more or less the same reasoning. If the company isn't doing well, he'll be like a field surgeon on the battlefield, able to take swift, and sometimes painful decisions, so as to allow the company to survive.

THE WORLD MY CHILDREN WILL INHERIT WILL BE MORE COMPETITIVE THAN THE ONE I DEALT WITH

What the **future** will be like in five words:

GLOBAL

Here, the leader must be open to a crystal-clear vision of what's going on in the world, consisting also of the study and analysis of customers, competitors, and possible macroeconomic phenomena: this allows you to decide if the strategy you use to engage the market will aim at a more global or local challenge, if the focus will be on one market or on several, where you believe you have a competitive edge.

DIGITAL

Elements affecting market development will include speed, and accessibility 24 hours a day, 365 days a year: in this situation it will be of fundamental importance to consider the power of information and data, the use of AI (artificial intelligence) as a support to understanding customers' preferences and thus guide the company to offer a more appropriate range of **INCREASINGLY PERSONALIZED PRODUCTS AND SERVICES**.

HUMAN

Nonetheless, I am alarmed by the sci-fi hypothesis of the computer replacing humankind completely. A computer doesn't have an empathetic view of the world; it is faster but perhaps less intuitive and colder. The machine may be perfect and superior to us as far as analysis is concerned, even in "predicting" the future, based as it is on mathematical models; through random simulations artificial intuition is able to make extremely complex elaborations, but they are and remain "artificial". A computer, for example, will not be able to convey the pathos of vision of a human heart **CONNECTED TO THE BRAIN**.

> The pressure exerted by emotion, the prodigious energy used to contract almost a hundred thousand times a day and circulate up to five liters of blood a minute, yes, that line alone might tell its story, outline its life, a life of flux and reflux, a life of valves opening and closing, a life of pulsations . . . that human heart, that same one, eludes the machines, no-one could claim to know it, and that night – a starless night, cold enough to crack the stones in the estuary and in the Pays de Caux, whilst a long wave devoid of reflections rolled up against the cliffs and the flat shape of the continent retreated revealing geological strata – that heart was returning the regular beat of an organ at rest, of a muscle that is slowly recharging – the pulse probably slower than fifty beats a minute – when the alarm of a cell phone went off at the foot of a narrow bed, on the touchscreen the echo of a sonar inscribed the figures 05.50 in glowing LEDs, and in that instant everything came crashing down.
>
> (Maylis de Kerangal, date)

THE HUMAN HEART connected to the brain which, at times, makes it possible to see things from a different perspective (the "more human human" that Friedrich Nietzsche spoke of) rather than what might be suggested by a simple past/future analysis.

COMPETITIVE

The world my children will inherit will be more competitive than the one I had to deal with: on the market there will be Indian geniuses, Chinese whizz-kids and the geographical barriers will be down, creating greater competition: this is why we shall need one of the characteristics we'll be talking about later – **fitness**. We shall have to train as hard as possible, whenever possible: muscle tone will be increasingly necessary to support talent; to use a sporting metaphor, we shall need to be able to integrate the human factor with building success, and I'm thinking here of that outstanding champion Roger Federer. In a sense we shall have to become war machines, as physically honed as Cristiano Ronaldo.

COMPASSIONATE

"Cooperation": in this complex world, those who don't cooperate are not **CLEAR** and will not manage to create a better world. We live in an age of sudden, quick change, and there are issues like sustainability and ecology that will become of ever greater strategical importance to everyone. What is certain, though, is that when I hear "by 2050" and consider that we are still in 2021, I feel like saying that perhaps we're being a bit presumptuous, and it's great to have a vision of ten years on, but of 30? First a few things must be changed. First we must act by supporting a few changes:

- zero emissions
- zero plastic

These mustn't turn into empty slogans or green washing. The changes must be accompanied by practical common sense if we don't want billions of people to end up ruined. We live in a GLOBAL ECONOMY, so rather than sustaining a quick switch, there must be the desire to ACT TOGETHER.

Change together.
To Be a Leader: Who Will Be the Leaders of Tomorrow?

As I see it, there will be **MORE WOMEN LEADERS** for three reasons:

1. It is only right that there should be more **APPRECIATION** for women's intelligence, intuition, and abilities than there has been so far, often due to socio-economic models linked to a past world that no longer exists.

2. Women are eminently capable of emerging on their own. This is why, when the issue of "pink quotas" is discussed, in theory, I immediately think of an archaic world: the most important thing is the freedom of human beings to express themselves and make choices so that we have a board or a team that is constituted by pink, black, yellow, and black quotas. I think this should be a factor that makes the difference to success. It shouldn't be a duty; not until we have complete freedom to choose and have a formula of **DIVERSITY WITHOUT OBLIGATIONS** will we really be living in the world of tomorrow.

3. Today's girls succeed in personifying the best of the perfect **MIX OF SUCCESS FACTORS** for the future: they're digitally literate, fit, put the data in order, think globally, are super (data-) driven in accessing information, and link this approach to human factors and pathos, through culture and empathy. In only a few years' time I believe we shall be able to reach a perfect balance between the older and younger generations. Partly because in terms of the dependence on technology that we have observed over the past few years, when I look at younger people I see them joking together, phone on the table, and they only take a look at it every now and then; they're no longer slaves to it (an average user touches the screen of their smartphone 2,000 times a day) while they talk, they're having fun, they're right there in the present, in the real world that also contains the technological tool. That little word "*also*" says it all.

I like to imagine there will be a return to the land, to the countryside, inland. To places where we shall rediscover a human dimension, without losing the global one. There's no going back.

We've acquired technology, the idea of being fit, of always keeping our eye on the ball and at the same time I believe that – after the pandemic that brought the world to a stop – we shall manage to find a way of being closer to the values that correspond most closely to us, of thinking and finally being ourselves. It's impossible to turn a blind eye.

THE LOST/REDISCOVERED TIME DOESN'T RETURN

Everything will depend on what we are able to do with this new criterion, intuition, appreciated for a year, or perhaps two. A micro-organism has taught us to win back the world of small things, the essential that's invisible to the eye. Shall we manage not to waste it all? To go on looking round us, be as courageous as we have been, choose where we want to be and live. Without pretending? It's always thanks to a space, a place, a habitat – home – that we recover time for ourselves.

RESTLESS, WITHOUT RESPITE, WITHOUT PAUSING THESE ARE THE ELEMENTS BY WHICH YOU CAN RECOGNIZE A LEADER, AS WELL AS THEIR SEARCH FOR A VISION, OF THE FUTURE, OF SUCCESS, OF THINGS WELL DONE

At the same time, this very American concept of *demanding with appreciation*, must be integrated with the ability to appreciate the waystages. The world is full of great managers and entrepreneurs who are not, however, capable of appreciation, of congratulating themselves, of enjoying the waystages, the positive things that happen while they're pursuing an objective. As I see it, not being able to seize the moment is a serious lack in a leader.

IF YOU MANAGE TO CREATE EMPATHY WITH YOUR "TROOPS", IF YOU'VE SUCCEEDED IN MOTIVATING THEM EVEN IN THE WORST AND THE MOST CRITICAL OF MOMENTS, WHEN THEY THINK OF YOU, THEY WILL DO SO WITH A SMILE AND WITH ESTEEM, GRATITUDE, AND AFFECTION

Because first and foremost you will have conveyed the sense of what it is to be human. Whether they remain in the same position all their life or decide to go elsewhere, the leader will always be able to leave (more than) something in the minds and hearts of the people they encountered.

To have **VISION** also means

- knowing the moves to be made when you want to start new companies or departments;
- knowing what you want to offer but also what you don't want to offer;
- knowing the service offer and helping the company to monetize the value offered to customers (lever of pricing, definition of revenue models for capturing the customers' willingness to pay, a clear focus on price management).

The difference between a leader and a great manager is that a leader recognizes the value of gratitude, including the gratitude that others have shown towards them. If you can't see it, you can't convey it.

Personally, in my career there were two essential turning points regarding two lessons in particular:

1. one regarded **METHOD**;
2. the other regarded **OPPORTUNITY**.

1. In high school, when I was 15, a teacher taught me how to organize my studiZes: she was a nun; I went to a private school. Every day, she selected those who were to be tested completely at random, by pulling names out of a hat. This "lottery" happened regularly so that you might even get tested for five days in a row. **LUCK HAS ITS OWN LOGIC**: for me it was a great lesson, which then set the basis for my university studies and future exams. It got me used to being prepared the whole time, instead of only on demand, to counting on my own resources, to obtaining the appreciation of the person listening to me, being competent, each time raising the bar for the next objective.
2. When my father died, I was 23, and my mother and I were left alone. First came the feeling of annihilation; death is natural, but what can you say . . . Tears, the ocean within you, the life you'd known up to then somehow vanishes, it's the first seismic tremor in your inner world, a wormhole in the stomach that each of us tries to heal as best we can. The void. But then you rebuild yourself. **THE SILENCE TURNS INTO A GAZE TOWARDS THE HORIZON. YOU MUST PUSH ON.** Little by little I got back on my feet, though some events mark you forever – we're constellations of pain overcome – and it was then that the father of my best friend, who knew about my predicament, took me on in his insurance business. This was a turning point for me, **agnition**, the moment when my life changed: I was able to support myself while I studied, and that allowed me to graduate with honors, make a dream come true, and go on to study in the United States, keeping the promise made to my father.

Leader Building *or* How Do You Build a Leader?

Suppose leadership were a genetic code in a person's DNA?

Suppose leadership were a way of being as well as doing?

In general, it might even be said that a leader possesses certain typical characteristics:

1. They are **COMPETITIVE**: in a sense, leadership can be compared to a sport requiring endurance, in which you need great mental and physical stamina. A leader is fit, tough, and focused: if they were a sportsperson, the leader would be a long-distance runner but one who was also capable of sprinting to put a distance between themselves and the other runners.

2. **RESTLESS WITH APPRECIATION**: the leader is continually searching for what's "good" because they know that good is better than best, and that's why they are always on the move. Perfection comes by chance. They appreciate beauty, allow the right amount of time for their players to celebrate their victories and enjoy life – "work hard, play hard" – when guiding a team they make concessions. They don't adopt a hierarchy, the true leader knows that it's only a matter of having different roles at a given time. They are like the trainer of a football team who aims at having the team play a perfect game. They manage people rather than roles: like Joseph Pep Guardiola or Carlo Ancelotti, who can balance the human aspects of their teams as well as the technical, or Jose´ Mourinho, too.

3. **EMPATHETIC AND UNDERSTANDS THINGS BY USING SOCIAL + EMOTIONAL INTELLIGENCE:** they have to try and understand how to get the best out of the team. Their secret is always to be a good companion, to make the most of strong points and help recover weaknesses, criticize at the right time, and encourage, always lovingly. They convey the broad vision to the others, as though saying, by means of their attitude, **we are a team**; even in difficult moments they stop to listen or have constructive discussions; being a team means being a wedge for splitting defenses apart, breaking down levees, keeping things together.

4. **COURAGEOUS**: they are not afraid of the challenges that appear, nor do they fear what they are not acquainted with but know that they will have to learn what they don't know (yet). They want to travel new paths, is an explorer in their own way, chooses paths that have perhaps never been explored before, is capable of guiding themselves and the

team through the forests without getting reckless or ignoring danger. On the contrary, with courage they accept changes and faces them with analysis and instinct day by day.

Gandhi, for example, was a courageous leader because he knew that by moving the masses he himself would be running a risk, his freedom and his life, for an objective.

Yet he was ready to do so. Because when you are at the helm and face up to changes, you must do so first and foremost by your own example. This is what the naval commander does on board a ship which finds itself dealing with different weather every day, so that the crossing takes varying lengths of time and that must be got used to; *each day is unexpected.*

Good is better than the best.
The leader is always on the move.
Perfection comes by chance.

Vision | Steve Jobs
Conductor of an orchestra

Inside a garage he created the future.

Genial, ferocious, perfectionist, passionate, entrepreneur, revolutionary.

Trying to define Steve Jobs would be like trying to eat pizza with a teaspoon.

Whilst common mortals were trying to understand how to do business, Jobs developed the concept of invention, changing the world to its utmost.

A loner, abrupt, irritable, and at times even unpleasant, he had more confidence in his intuition than in his own shadow – a leader capable of making his ideas into a global icon.

His intuition made him unique.

Jobs was the first to understand that in the digital age, value is to be obtained by combining technology with creativity, innovation, and imagination. Without the fear that other people may fail to understand.

Open, never rigid, a free thinker, Jobs made honesty and truth into the mainstays of his way of understanding leadership.

A wizard of communication but not at all empathetic, obsessive, controlled, diabolically dual, almost magical in his inspirational talks that won over thousands of people and later millions of users in the four corners of the planet. With his aesthetically attractive products, he has succeeded in bringing to market minimal design applied to usability.

Raised as an adopted child amongst the pioneers of IT, Jobs has demonstrated to twenty-first-century humankind that everything is interconnected – just like hardware and software – nothing is all black or all white, but everything is integrated, like the Apple world, a symbol of our times, that made him famous.

A complex personality, mystical (witness his travels in India in 1974), from the planet-wide boom of his creature right up to his illness, Jobs was the personification of the technological pioneer, spirit of adventure at all costs, based on an enterprising approach: "people don't know what they want, until you show them."

KEY TAKEAWAYS

"Our" leader

- has the ability to look further, as does their vision;
- follows their intuition and trusts their "gut feeling";
- manages things according to a "hypothesis first" and "MECE" approach;
- is able to change as events change;
- knows what the future is and what gratitude is (is a sportsperson, "restless with appreciation").

CHAPTER 4
Solitude/Dispensability

DOI: 10.4324/9781003378532-6

Solitude is a companion, a friend, that sometimes alarms us because it hides. Solitude is something that accompanies us throughout life. All of us.

However convinced we may be that we are sunny, open-minded people, however used to sharing we believe we are – after all we live in the age of social media and sharing – at key moments: "We're born alone, we live alone, we die alone. Only through our love and friendship can we create the illusion for the moment that we're not alone," said the great filmmaker Orson Welles. The same goes for all the decisions we take, which determine greater or lesser upheavals in our lives: for example, choosing to have a family, sharing our time with a companion. A leader is alone in the very same way.

Eventually we might conclude, a leader is "together with a team".

Because the leader is capable of listening to everyone and taking decisions that are shared as far as possible. Though there are situations in which an individual choice must be made. And this is the theme of "The Solitudine of Prime Numbers". When it's *time to pull the trigger*, as the Anglo-Saxons put it, for example – those are the moments you're on your own. Your decision will be made easier by the team, mitigated by analysis and study, pondered by the ability of the team members to enter into all the details that bear on the decision to be taken.

When you decide to respond to a request or a question, as best you can, whether your response is right or wrong, you should know that every choice is marked by solitude.

WHERE DO I GO WHEN I'M ALONE?

I don't have one particular place. But I tend to want a place where I can see the horizon and the sky. Where I can look up, talk to someone who can help me think: to my parents or, better, someone I think might somehow be my guiding light. Always knowing that in the end it will be me, with my analyses and study, and after consulting the people I esteem and love, and who esteem and love me, who chooses between apparently conflicting solutions. Instinct plays its part.

A blue sky offers me a dimension that helps me make more serene choices.

If I had to choose a place, I'd say it would be those huge open spaces in the United States with only a few houses scattered here and there, enormous forests all around and the mountains of Utah or New Hampshire, or Montana, or Massachusetts in the background.

Though, it could actually be the skies over Sardinia!

Everything in life is connected.

Our days, the mud, the recoveries, the climbs, friends, breathlessness, brioches for breakfast. Clouds. What you see. And have touched. The stuff dreams are made of, your words, what you believe in.

> **At times the laws make things round "and" square at the same time, at others, fate or superstition step in but in the end the gods do what they wish with humankind.**

Draw on all the experiences you can before you *pull the trigger.*

Solitude | Sergio Marchionne
Entrepreneur

If you come from a little place in Abruzzo, with sheep grazing on the green, porous rocks, what will they call you when you grow up?

Sergio's father was called Concezio, and he was a Marshall of the Carabinieri during the Second World War. When Sergio was 14, the Marchionne family decided to immigrate to Canada, where a sister of his mother's had already settled.

You were an immigrant and not even a middle-class child. The world shouldn't have expected anything of you. Yet first you graduated in philosophy and then in law.

Sometimes the laws make things round "and" square at the same time; for others, fate or superstition steps in, but in the end, the gods do what they wish with humankind.

Audaces fortuna iuvat in Latin means "fortune generally favors those who face risk with courage". And that's just how it was.

After graduating and obtaining a masters in business administration (MBA), Marchionne was appointed to several prestigious positions first in Canada and then in Switzerland, chosen by Umberto Agnelli as a board member of the Lingotto automobile company, and then, in June 2004, he became CEO of the FIAT group, FIAT being the acronym of *Fabbrica Italiana Automobili Torino* (Italian Automobile Factory of Turin).

The little immigrant's leadership model is the child of his hunger for success, and this is how in 2009 Sergio Marchionne was to scale the heights of the Chrysler company, to acquire 20% of the American giant, negotiating directly with Barack Obama, the newly elected president of the United States of America. And so FCA came into being: 4.5 million automobiles a year, the world's seventh largest automobile producer. Before the pandemic. Before the fossil world collapsed beneath the blows dealt by an organism measuring between 50 and 140 nanometers.

Then, in 2014, Marchionne was to become president of Ferrari, replacing Luca Cordero di Montezemolo.

The images of some of his most famous handshakes have gone down in history: Michael Schumacher, Pope Benedict XVI, Bernie Ecclestone, Sergio Mattarella. He died in 2018, afteryears of medical treatment, without ever having spoken of his illness. With him he wanted only his children and his second wife.

Marchionne was a leader whose ruthless vision, together with the utmost reserve about his private life, produced a **brand**: both Italian and international, able to combine the mission of the private sector with negotiation, and even compromise with the public.

THE PRIME NUMBERS OF THE LEADER

One of the things you learn is to live with yourself: with the time you devote to yourself and to the people you love; you manage to make time for yourself, your family, your friends, and everything that recharges you.

(MY) STRONG POINTS

A leader is a **good man** who acts on what they think, according to their values and sentiments; they are a person who possesses a **complete set** of managerial and analytical tools and who values creativity and the practice of delegating.

(MY) WEAK POINTS

There comes a moment when you feel the almost obsessive need for constant reports, to hang on to the illusion of control. Otherwise your level of **anxiety** grows. Not out of lack of trust. But rather, to make sure you're still moving forward. In this sense, the leader is the father/mother of their own story. They make choices, keeps themselves informed, gives back in return. As we would say to a child who's a long way from home: "Let me know where you are and where you're thinking of going." And if, in my opinion, it's best not to set out on a certain path, I'll ask directly, "Why do you want to go there?" and I may persuade myself of the opposite and alter my position, because **A LEADER CAN LISTEN AND HAVE DOUBTS, EVEN ABOUT THEMSELVES**, never becomes enamored of their personal opinion, but makes judgements on individual occasions. And this is the point: I need to be informed, to enter selectively into the details of every choice, to understand what direction it's going in, but at the same time I am open-minded.

LEADERSHIP IS BEING AVAILABLE 24/7. There is never a moment when a father is not available to his children! At the same time, you mustn't be there at every moment of the decision-making process, making your authority felt or having it acknowledged.

Indeed, here there is a fundamental concept to remember – that of

Being dispensable.

A leader must be dispensable. The moment I realize I'm indispensable, I'm aware I'm doing a bad job for my stakeholders and for those who work for me, by creating a relationship of dependence.

Instead, a leader has achieved the utmost if they can transmit their way of being to the people who are working on the project and on their vision.

In the uncertain times we live in, when you know where you are today but tomorrow who knows, the only objective must be for everything to work. What is best is the enemy of what is good, we said. So everything must be able to work without the leader.

The leader must constitute the added value

The leader is simply a *primus inter pares*, an archetype, a function that I must cultivate both within myself and within the group. To be a leader, you always have to be completely focused.

Some people might interpret being dispensable as a passive element.

On the contrary, it's **ONLY BY BEING DISPENSABLE THAT THE LEADER KNOWS HOW TO GUIDE THEIR TEAM TO SURVIVAL AND CAN DO THIS EVEN WHEN THEY AREN'T THERE.**

A leader must be dispensable.

They must not be indispensable.

The leader must constitute the added value in a far vaster project.

The team must be free

The winning team is the one that has assimilated the trainer's plan and mood and then metabolized it and transformed it according to the characteristics of its individual elements. The leader's thinking is what must be conveyed. Each team member assimilates it as far as they can with the resources they have. And if the leader's concept is clear and permeable, each member of the team will make it their own. Then, and only then, will that concept come alive, transform itself, and start to exist thanks to the individual contributions that broaden its scope and allow all its possible implications to emerge.

A LEADER MUST BE FREE TO TAKE THEIR DECISIONS, TO SPEAK OPENLY WITH THE TEAM AND THE STAKEHOLDER, AND THINK HIS THOUGHTS THROUGH TO THE END

The concept of freedom is fundamental. The minute the leader feels constrained, they tend to break the leash and escape the harness, because you can't keep dreams in chains.

INDEPENDENCE, WITH RESPECT FOR YOUR OWN ROLE AND OBJECTIVES

Respect

Lastly, a leader must be intellectually free. And free to use their own intuition right to the end.

KNOWING HOW TO SAY NO IS FUNDAMENTAL

When you know you must pursue a long-term vision composed of several short-term objectives, situations may arise – suggested by others or by you yourself – in which it proves important to change your mind. Because that's what the direction imposes. Or else you realize that there are risks that haven't been considered in the bigger picture.

In those situations the only thing to do is admit to yourself: "I'm making a mistake, I must think again," call everything into question, even what has already been approved. Like starting over from zero. It takes courage. But only the person who's prepared to do it is a leader.

Thoughts are always on the move, and contexts change. When I make a business plan or deal with a company's strategic plan – and I believe every company and every person should have an idea of the direction they're moving in – that's when the world shifts. You draw up a plan at a precise time and take your decisions on a precise day. But the world will already have turned in another direction.

This is why a leader must be able to adapt, modify their analyses according to fluctuations in the economy, understand a person's **sentiments**, keep up to date with what's going on around them at a social and geopolitical level.

The leader is a person who manages to respond quickly and effectively to a changing world; they have a vision

There are waystages.

At times you have to overcome obstacles before reaching an aim; the basic idea doesn't change, but the path towards it does

FRIENDS AND ENEMIES

A leader's friend is whoever helps them to express themselves and is not envious of their success. This is true at all levels, whether we're talking about co-workers, bosses, or equals. Whoever helps the leader to express potential and intuition. In any way. Frankly pointing out mistakes, openly and sincerely. The proof is to be seen in loyalty, a fundamental concept. In the same way, criticism must be considered if it is constructive.

The enemies are those who say yes even when they don't agree and then withdraw their support, with cowardly negationism. They are the ones that undermine you. Because you will never have a real exchange. You will never have access to one of the most important vehicles: **THE TRUTH.** Bureaucracy, for example, is a "thing" to fight in a company as well as in politics; you can decide what you like, but if the structure doesn't work, everything will grind to a halt.

In the macrocosm, the writer Franz Kafka was right: bureaucracy is humankind's enemy, the rules that turn into walls and prisons. Structures that slow down work instead of promoting it. People who hide behind smiles and turn out to be disloyal, false, closed, are a leader's enemies. The ones who tend to cage you behind fences or in enclosures that are not yours. And from which you must always break free.

CHANGE

We are living in a time of great change. The world is moving faster and faster. The rhythm is more and more demanding. This is what gives rise to the need, the importance, of keeping fit.

Make things happen.

These changes need people with considerable mental flexibility, who demonstrate that they are not rigid and don't base their suppositions on ready-made theories, for example, of how a team should be managed or how you should dress or what your professional training should be, the necessary and adequate *ratio studiorum* that allows you to do certain work. These are concepts that were fine up to a few years ago, perhaps. But today things need to be evaluated as and when they come up.

Change is a relentless concept that takes you in search of knowledge and forces you to constantly check your objectives according to the resources you have and the means the shareholders allow you. It must be tackled without preconceived itineraries, using history and everything else that has preceded it. At the same time training is necessary to keep **fit enough for the role you take on**, the hat you decide to wear.

And here the new technologies and digital tools, as well as the new techniques of management, are indispensable elements for a leader. For example, central concepts are to be

Data-driven + 80/20

DATA-DRIVEN means being guided by information, by data. On the basis of this data, taking decisions that are syntheses but based on actual quantitative analyses and therefore pondered. Having said this, I believe that one of Pareto's principles applies here, that is, that 80% of answers come from 20% of the analysis and that the time must be taken to obtain the most effective response in that precise moment, with the kit of information available, net of the information asymmetry that is never known, especially on the market, until it's too late.

A leader must be able to respond efficiently to change. This is why they are the person responsible for making decisions. If, in order to do so, they got lost in the analyses, they would be brought to a standstill.

"The search for what's best is *always* an enemy of what's good."

When you're a leader, you must be able to obtain what's good and immediately afterwards
move on to the next step

The right balance for a leader is to be guided by analyses, which, however, must be the tools of support for intuition.

RESEARCH AND TALENT GARDENING are of absolute importance to a leader. Talent is something innate, but it has to be accompanied. Talent, for example, belongs to the person who is searching for the utmost, the best, perfection, but without letting themselves be brought to a standstill. Talent is ageless. It can be found in young people and in older ones, who perhaps find themselves excluded from the job market today. Talent must be sought amongst the new generations as amongst the 50 to 60-year-olds. The talented are *rough diamonds*, hidden jewels, to be protected on the one hand and drawn out to the full on the other. It's a delicate, subterranean balance.

The formula for talent is a combination of

energy + new vision + experience + maturity

Talent must be sought both inside and outside your own company. On one hand, those already inside your community must be made the most of, and at the same time it's necessary to keep an eye on what's going on outside, which is part of looking **beyond**. The motivation of these talents must be observed as well as their drive, so that people can grow, understanding their potential for development, putting their commitment to the test **when they are part of the project**, so that they can then be included in all the new contexts that are generated by the initial idea.

What's more, it's important to have a method and an organization in place that is constantly able to get hold of interesting new talent to introduce into your own organization today or tomorrow.

CORPORATE ENVIRONMENT

The company is a habitat.

It forms us, particularly when we are young and need to set the bases for all that will come later. It gives us the first 100 words we learn and on which we build all that will be in the future. It is no coincidence that some great schools of management exist: from the multinationals to general consultancy firms like Bain & Company – leaders in performance improvement, Procter & Gamble, Coca-Cola; right up to the investment banks like Goldman Sachs and Morgan Stanley.

A company can convey a *forma mentis* to the people who work on a project or the **CORE PEOPLE**, in other words the basic competences: excellence, **WORK HARD, PLAY HARD**, the work ethic, shared values obviously declined according to the context, which might be the possibility of smart working for tech companies in California, or going halfway to meet the demands of creative freedom, where the job doesn't foresee "clocking in or clocking out".

And so the core values are marked by **SPECIFICS AND BY FLEXIBILITY**, according to the role involved. Companies' knowledge assets are mental infrastructures: figures, historical data, or the things that have already been done and from which best practice may be extrapolated, for example. For instance, I suggest keeping an archive on the company's knowledge data so that people with tasks to perform can refer to internal expertise, those dealing with the launch of new products, or those managing communication will have firm landmarks to refer to with respect to their own positions. Practical examples that are often worth a thousand theories.

The real "teaching" companies are those where you find
culture strength muscle tone organization and talent gardening

We are dispensable.
Everyone must move forward.
And will do so.

Being dispensable | Mary Barra
Entrepreneur

The first woman to become CEO of one of the Big Three American automobile producers, Mary Barra has been CEO of GM (General Motors) since 2014. She has been on the board of directors of Disney since 2017 and since 2020 on the board of Stanford University.

From a family of Finnish origin, her real family name is Mäkelä. Her grandparents moved to Minnesota, in the heart of the Midwest, and her father, Ray, was born in Michigan.

Perhaps it was for the trees that the first settlers, the emigrants from northern Europe, chose America.

The *Land of Dreams* or *Land of Tomorrow*.

In any case, endless horizons, trees as far as the eye could see, amongst the confederation's vastest stretches of prairie to remain intact.

"We're of little consequence compared to the Earth, which will go on without us." This is what Mary must have inherited from the habitat she grew up in, the great lesson being: you die and tomorrow the sun will rise all the same.

We are dispensable. Everything must go on. And it will.

After a degree obtained at the General Motors Institute (today University of Kettering), Mary became a member of the Engineering Honor Society Tau Beta Pi ΤΒΠ, the second oldest in the United States, which over the years has produced some of the most important figures in our contemporary world: Buzz Aldrin (astronaut, second man to set foot on the Moon), Michael Bloomberg (economist, Mayor of New York City), and Jeff "Mr. Amazon" Bezos.

Even as a young woman, Barra began to reveal the gift of a high intellectual profile and great competence, combined with admirable devotion to work, as for example when she was 18 and entered GM as a student on a cooperative program known simply as "co-op", which offers academic credits for job experience in a perspective of so-called school-work continuity.

A vertically formed leader, over time Mary Barra was able to climb to the heights of the company thanks to a highly innovative method, for example, by leading GM towards the production of electric, driverless cars (in 2017 GM was already starting to launch the Chevy Bolt EV onto the market. Declared autonomy: over 300 kilometers, bettering rivals like Tesla in the race to produce the first electric cars at a price under $40,000).

Mary, like Angela Merkel, is known by her husband Tony Barra's family name and is the type of leader known above all for her strategic positions, on which she has worked both professionally and from a human perspective, for example by looking for solutions to end the gender gap in the company. It is thanks to her that GM constantly wins high credit in "equality" reporting: in 2018, GM was one of the two companies – globally – that had no gender pay-gap discrimination.

KEY TAKEAWAYS

"Our" leader

- can accept the fact that every choice is marked by solitude;
- draws on all possible experience before "pulling the trigger";
- acts on what they think and is available 24/7;
- makes themselves dispensable, wishing to be the added value;
- has "fit", "make it happen", and "move on to the next one" as the mantras in their mindset;
- takes data-driven decisions.

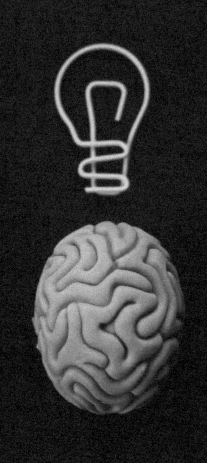

CHAPTER 5

Style, communication, *un*popularity, higher education

DOI: 10.4324/9781003378532-7

A leader's vision must be communicated as widely as possible.

At the same time, it should be no problem to be perceived at times as an asshole leader, the one many manuals describe, without mincing their words, as a hardliner, an XXX-head. By definition the leader's vision is that of **CAPTAIN MY CAPTAIN** – as in the film *Dead Poets' Society*, the words being taken from the poem that the great American writer Walt Whitman wrote on the death of President Abraham Lincoln – one man alone commanding the ship. A leader's thought cannot and must never strive for complete consensus; sooner or later someone will dissatisfy them, and that is the whole point. The firm awareness and acceptance of this responsibility.

I think it is also necessary to distinguish between great social issues – on which, given this premise, the utmost consensus should be sought – and purely corporate issues, on which instead the consensus of the stakeholders should be sought.

EVERY LEADER MUST FIND THEIR OWN STYLE

Based on the facts and on the validity of their own vision. The wider the audience, the more empathetic the communication of the message should be. The **STAGES** the change goes through are a different matter and should be communicated in a "sympathetic" rather than merely empathetic manner so that they become effective and are well received. In fact, the first reaction human beings have when faced with change is closure: so that what a leader has to do, instead, is make all aspects of it positive, anticipating the typical regressive psychology of emotional reactions.

Then there is another issue, that is, **WHEN IT IS THE LEADER THAT HAS TO SAY NO**. In this case the "no" must be correctly communicated. It must be firm and motivated. Their position must be presented as necessary and may even prove to be unpopular. When you're looking for excellence, the most important thing is to support the direction of your vision and/or of the change. A leader encourages change, and if someone in the team doesn't push hard enough, an assertive attitude must be maintained.

assertive
/as·ser·tive/ adjective
refers to a person capable of showing their worth whilst respecting the rights of others

Not everyone is suited to all tasks, or to all companies. Some may excel in other projects, but perhaps not in ours, or vice versa. The real point is to manage to decline everything in the best way for a company, ours. The search for popularity at all costs is typical of a politician, not a leader.

A leader seeks **popularity for his vision,** not his own **popularity,** from others.

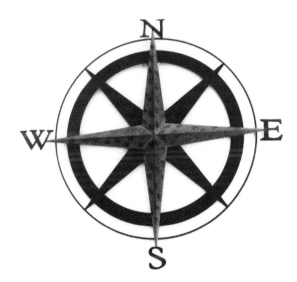

The more popular/shareable a vision is and the more appreciably empathetic is the way it is communicated, the more feasible the decision will become. It is as if there were a sort of sum total of hours in terms of visions and ideas: the change is introduced and then broken down into successive steps, in which what has already been achieved goes on to accumulate with the next step. Some concepts need a considerable budget, others bold communication. Some visions need to be protected; others need basic consensus to be built. Always bearing in mind

WHAT CAN BE OBTAINED *VERSUS* WHAT CANNOT BE OBTAINED

Lastly, when decisions are taken, the possible side effects should be considered. This means that **KNOWING YOU DON'T KNOW**, that Plato quotes with respect to Socrates, that is, "an awareness of not knowing definitely, which does, however, become the basic motor force of the desire to know."

It's a fine thing to talk of "sustainability", of epoch-making changes, but first, far more realistically, I have to make a transition towards them – waystages in the approach, so to speak – otherwise we remain in the realm of *wannabe* with no basis for their implementation.

IF THE LEADER WERE A FAMOUS PERSON, they might be the king of the Spartans, Leonidas.

Or Jose´ Mourinho, who gives his all for his team and uses all he can, even his (own) unpopularity. What does Mourinho do? He communicates aggressively so as to create a protective barrier around his team and the club. **HE REMOVES AND TAKES ONTO HIS OWN SHOULDERS ALL THAT MIGHT "HARM" THE TEAM AND THE MANAGEMENT. THE LEADER IS HIS VISION,** and this is why, whatever opinion one may have, in terms of communication Mourinho is a great leader for his team, and that's what counts!

A true leader draws the enemy fire: "I'm the one responsible," they say. And again,

> If you do things wrong, the mistake is yours but it's mine, too, to the extent that I failed to understand. Perhaps you should have asked for help but I take the responsibility for not having realized in time and found a solution by making the necessary changes.

In this sense Mourinho personifies the spirit of **CROSSING THE FOREST TOGETHER**. A leader must point out the right path. Not everyone is necessarily able to follow it, though. And in this case, *it's never personal*: if needs be, the leader can (also) be tough with his players, for example, if they aren't fit enough. What they can do is accompany them towards other experiences.

These are the occasions on which the **SOLITUDE OF THE LEADER** makes itself felt: the leader's priority is to be able to manage any situation, if they have to make replacements ten minutes from the final whistle, then they will. Because this is what the outcome of the game depends on.

The leader is a frontman; they must be accountable.

To pursue the football metaphor, Megan Rapinoe comes to mind – captain of the US women's football team that won the World Cup in 2019. Rapinoe's spirit was responsible for a collective identity being created. This is how the #USWNT, the US national women's football team, became the fruit of a winning mentality:

- on the field: in the team all members have the same objectives (and there are no ulterior motives), and every team member is placed in the position of being able to play in the "right" position;
- off the field: the discussion on equal pay for men and women is encouraged – the so-called gender gap – and on LGBTQ+ rights.

From the figure of Megan Rapinoe, we can extrapolate a few rules about leadership:

- if and when a leader **TAKES A STAND, THEY BELIEVE IN IT RIGHT TO THE END**;
- they are **HONEST**, and THEIR words are the expression of the actions they perform;
- **THEY ARE ALWAYS THERE FOR EVERYONE.** The leaders are the first to be ready for the fray if anyone on the outside attacks a team member. In addition, they encourage and are always on the front line, guiding the attack;
- a leader **DEFENDS THEIR IDEAs** in the sense that they rely on their own judgement, after a complex procedure of balancing general information and processes of self-awareness;
- real leaders are not only able to achieve results and change the world for the better thanks to their opinions, even "radical" ones, but if they are **PUT UNDER PRESSURE, THEY GIVE THEIR BEST AND BRING HOME THE RESULT.**

Lastly.

If leadership were a person, it would be Mario Draghi. Draghi has had a **POWERFUL** career.

Everyone remembers his famous words as governor of the European Central Bank in the 2012 conference after the Eurozone crisis in 2010: "Whatever it takes", in terms both of results and of country image, or of **REPUTATION**. The assumption of that responsibility was the embodiment of "drawing enemy fire", like Leonidas at Thermopylae and, at the same time, accepting **UNPOPULARITY**, like Mourinho. Draghi acted the same way when he accepted the appointment as prime minister of Italy, and in this role, he discreetly replaced people from the previous government. We are talking here of Draghi the economist, banker, public administrator: his *physique du rôle* is the embodiment of the leader with a vision, and when he comes across things he judges "of no use", he replaces them with the "most appropriate response possible".

I believe that Italy and Germany, under Angela Merkel, have had the best government leaders in the world in terms of competence, assertiveness, charisma, political inclusivity, and the ability to listen and mediate: in his role, Draghi has proved capable of keeping almost all political factions in the government, taking it upon himself to decide on the crucial issues. This has been possible thanks to the credibility he has created in the field, both at home and internationally, and both in the European public space and in the private one of the great investment banks. As well as this, the following he has makes all the difference, the **LOYAL TEAM OF PEOPLE** built up over the years; for example, there was talk of the *Draghi boys*, a group of young talents from the Harvard Business School and the other most important schools in the world at the time he was Governor of the ECB. And this is one of the **KEYS TO THE SUCCESS OF A LEADER**: having champions – the 50 Argonaut heroes – in the right places.

Managing to be dispensable
[not being afraid]
having the best people in your team
[each in their specific role]
Only in this way can a leader think of obtaining GREAT RESULTS.

"But there is another message I want to tell you. Within our mandate, the ECB is ready to do whatever it takes to preserve the euro. And believe me, it will be enough." *Mario Draghi*

As they say where I come from, in communication **YOU HAVE TO BE ABLE TO PLAY THE HEEL-AND-TOE MOVE. COMMUNICATION IS A TOOL FOR ACHIEVING YOUR OBJECTIVE.**

If I have to motivate the team, I show them the glass half full. If instead the company is doing well but not well enough, the glass will be half empty: this means that there are (still) objectives to reach. The game isn't over. There's (more) work to be done. Communication depends on *momentum*, in turn linked to a route and to the characteristics of *that particular* audience.

WE MUST ALWAYS ASK OURSELVES WHAT WE ARE COMMUNICATING AND TO WHOM

"The medium is the message."

wrote Marshall McLuhan, the Canadian philosopher, sociologist, and theorist of communication, who in the mid-sixties anticipated the debate on communication in the age of Internet and the social networks with this important declaration, stressing the importance of the means of communication rather than the message.

A prime example is what happened after publication of the extended edition of the 1967 *The Medium Is the Message*, where the word **MESSAGE** was replaced on the cover (!) at the printers, by the word **MASSAGE**. In this situation, instead of hastening to cover up the mistake, McLuhan transformed the event into a bulwark of his own thought: he declared that the mistake had been made on purpose and was to be understood as **MESS AGE** "the age of chaos", and **MASS AGE**, "the age of the masses".

PRICE, IDENTITY, RESULTS, QUANTITY: WHAT DOES IT MEAN TO BE POPULAR?

A leader is popular if/when their leadership is accompanied by two elements:

- **RESULTS**: a leader doesn't merely have a vision but acts, otherwise their leadership is an illusion;
- when there are **PEOPLE** ready to follow them.

Whatever the case, a manager will be spoken of both well and badly, and this, too, is a fact.

There will always be flatterers and detractors, but the one important thing is that there are people ready to follow them and a front consisting of people that esteem them. Leadership foresees a substrata, an army, a

BAND OF RENEGADES who would give their lives, and are willing to run the race alongside them. Wherever they go.

Being a maker of your own context
Half and half
By heart

You must know if something is **DOABLE**, have a clear understanding of what is doable, pragmatically achievable. You must put the present into context, understand where you want to go, what you can do *hic et nunc*, here and now (company building is not a Pindaric flight). There must be a practical basis, ability to estimate what can be done, step by step, towards which objective, and on the basis of which vision.

And then.

You have to be clear about the macroeconomic context you're moving in, know the political environment and infrastructure, as well as the KPI (key performance indicators) – general indicators, of quality, cost of service (or time) – which are keys to be monitored and applied to every initiative. These indicators are both financial – data-yielding engines of income, profitability, capital invested, financial sustainability – and human: ability to perform, the team effort towards achieving a relative objective.

Make it happen.

Never losing sight of a vision of what is best and the achievement of what is good, on the 80/20 basis.

Improvise.

Improvising instead means guessing the route, assuming "I am here". Asking yourself "what's the next step?" And here there's an element of intuition. You must be able to manage the infinite problems and have a perfect knowledge of the implications of **THE COMBINED DIFFICULTIES/OPPORTUNITIES**, because as soon as you take any decision, *panta rei*, everything flows, the world is on the move: the business plan is fine today, tomorrow who knows. There is a path to go down, decisions must be made as to what makes it possible to reach the objective, and in a sense they have not been planned but represent the subsequent stages on a possible route. In this sense, the long term consists equally of vision and decisions.

Leaders are capable of changing the world.

THE IMPORTANCE OF THE BEST SCHOOLS

Schools act on one of the most important levels for the development of leadership, that is, on the individual level. This means the shaping + vision of where you want to get to. It is during your school career that the talents you want to develop are established, as well as the weaknesses you have to manage. In Anglo-Saxon culture education and higher education are fundamental: in Italy only those who graduate with 110 and honors can go on to study in the United States at a top American business school (this is where, to date, the elites of management are formed in business education).

Ivy League: this is the title that embraces the eight most prestigious (elite) private universities in the United States:

- Yale University
- Harvard University
- University of Pennsylvania
- Brown University
- Princeton University
- Columbia University
- Dartmouth College
- Cornell University

Everything about this concept of school is grandiose: the buildings, the gardens, the echo of every stone evoking stories – *Dead Poets' Society, Animal House*. There are numerous titles that tell the stories of these American schools (even *This Side of Paradise* by Francis Scott Fitzgerald, *The Great Gatsby*), some focusing more on the ludic side of daily life, others telling stories of higher education, or of investment bankers.

Taking a look at the confraternities, life on campus, it seems incredible that kids of 17–18 should be able to go to university and work at the same time. Today, in evaluating the CV of a young person applying for a job, the first thing to look at is their educational career. There are the high performers who look for excellence in their marks. At the same time, what are they "outside" the academic world? If instead of being a waitress/waiter in a restaurant, a young person has spent a year in Canada or Switzerland, or worked as an assistant, this can be a clue. Another absolute value is intellectual curiosity. Competitive sportsmanship, being fit, is as important as wanting to take life by storm, learning, being hungry for life.

> I went to the woods because I wished to live deliberately, to front only the essential facts of life, and see if I could not learn what it had to teach, and not, when I came to die, discover that I had not lived. I did not wish to live what was not life, living is so dear; nor did I wish to practise resignation, unless it was quite necessary. I wanted to live deep and suck out all the marrow of life, to live so sturdily and Spartan-like as to put to rout all that was not life, to cut a broad swath and shave close, to drive life into a corner, and reduce it to its lowest terms.
>
> (Henry David Thoreau, 2017)

In the States the post-college level is *very demanding*. You sleep very little, you have courses in the morning, you study alone in the afternoon, whilst in the evening there are study groups right up to 1:00 a.m. It's a cross-cultural world, a perfect mix of Americans, Europeans, Asians, where different sorts of competition coexist. It's of basic importance to get acquainted with different cultures and not only from an academic point of view. Being able to deal with **CROSS-CULTURAL COMMUNICATION** is an immediate way into the swiftly moving, global world and helps you understand people's logic outside preestablished schemes, because you meet them in their own habitat, with their original language, their culture, the place they come from, what they cook, what they think, how they eat.

This is how you learn to build, **BUILD THE WORLD, WITH THE "RIGHT" WORDS,** which will then form thoughts. The switch comes a few years later, when you change from thinking in your original language and then perhaps translating, into thinking directly in English. The point is to realize that there are various ways of doing business, and that to guide people, in the end the old saying still holds: "When in Rome, do as the Romans do."

It's important to have **A ROUTE TO LEADERSHIP THAT ADAPTS** to different cultures, and this is the only way you will be

- ready and prepared to respond adequately to change;
- mentally and practically capable of responding openly and in a flexible way to the demands of a world on the move.

Batman is a solitary superhero who has confidence in the excellence of his collaborators.

Style, communication, *un*popularity, higher education | Batman
Superhero

When his parents are murdered before his very eyes, little Bruce Wayne knows his destiny. This is how one of the richest orphans in the history of comic strips is to become the *Dark Horseman*: Batman.

A character that started out in 1939 in the *Detective Comics*, Batman has evolved over time: films, TV series in the sixties, animated films, even to becoming an icon of Lego. Batman has come down to us over the years, right up to the *Dark Knight* version by the brilliant director Christopher Nolan, and sealed his fame as one of the best-loved superheroes ever, although he isn't a real superhero at all. Batman doesn't have superpowers, he isn't an alien like Superman, nor the prince of the oceans like Aquaman, nor the Queen of the Amazons, Wonder Woman's "colleague", all belonging to the world of DC Comics (publisher of US comic strips and amongst the most important worldwide, together with Marvel). Batman is a man who enhances his body and trains it to fight and to resist, with the help of money – money is a means, however, never an end in itself – and he has arms and equipment made, with which he fights and defeats evil.

After the death of his father, a philanthropist and architect, young Bruce comes to the psychological watershed that will lead him to be a vigilante, the guard of Gotham City, a lone leader, yet eminently human. Bruce Wayne the millionaire becomes Batman on the day he returns from the cave full of bats that had terrorized him as a child: "Embrace your worst fear. Become one with the darkness. Focus. Concentrate! Govern your senses," Ducard will advise him in the first film of Nolan's trilogy, *Batman Begins*.

Don't be afraid. Do all you can to reach your objective. Make sacrifices.

Batman is a lonely superhero who trusts in the excellence of his collaborators, in particular his supporter Robin, the wonder boy; Lucius Fox, the inventor of the family business; and above all Alfred, who is not only his butler but in time becomes a business partner, a friend, a confidant, in a way even a father figure.

KEY TAKEAWAYS

"Our" leader

- does not pursue the objective of total consensus;
- can communicate empathetically, effectively, at times also assertively;
- practices accountability in decisions, assuming the responsibility for their team;
- knows the best schools (universities, companies, consulting firms, life experience) and is capable of appreciating formation and talent;
- seeks "hunger" for life, success, knowledge, etc. in people.

PART II

Horizon

Feet on the ground, variable
geographies, and real dreams

CHAPTER 6

Foundations

DOI: 10.4324/9781003378532-9

WHAT IS GROUNDING?

The basic elements we are made up of are words, forms, objects, and the work we do or try to do as well as we can, curiosity and being ready for the changing world.

Ourselves changing "with" the world. Ourselves being able to change the world.

LOVE

If a leader doesn't love, they will be incomplete. Someone who can't convey love will be the leader of a team they don't feel passionate about, and in which they cannot be truly empathetic. Even if a team is "perfect", when difficulties arise – and sooner or later they will – the leader will not be able to keep it with them because they don't know what keeps a family together, in the broadest sense of the word "family", which here includes, for example, the group working on a **PROJECT**, which then dissolves when the latter has been completed; four best friends; four men roped together climbing a mountain with crampons, belted round the waist to walls of ice that might swallow them from one moment to the next; family is *your dog*, the family lexicon that joins you to the others: "Home is not *where* you are but who you're with," writes Linda Faas, the leading Scandinavian illustrator.

Sentiments, kindness, caresses, hugs, smiles, understanding mistakes, acknowledging you're not perfect.

Love is being able to give and ask with your heart, not only with your mind.

LOYALTY

If a leader is not loyal, how can they imagine their team wants, or is able, to fight together and alongside one another? Knowing that they don't share the same feelings towards the team, will they really be fighting with them and for them? Leadership means displaying complete transparency, having a shared agenda made up of **SACRIFICE**: training, working hard, studying, using your own time because you're devoting it to the project, and to shared objectives, being able to give up something for an objective that's bigger than you are. Not unless you sacrifice yourself can you demand the same commitment from others, in this sense the leadership relationship is based on **MUTUAL COMMITMENT**, and yet you must practice and teach independence: this is where courage is born – at the last minute you may discover you're facing the unknown all alone, you may fail and get things wrong, yet this is all part of the game. **THAT'S LEADERSHIP, BABY!** (Borrowing from the title of the film inspired by what actually happened to the daily paper *New York World* after the death of Joseph Pulitzer.)

> In English there are two words for the concept of "being alone".
>
> Solitude is the word for positive, well-aware aloneness, that drives us to create enough space around us, so that we have room to think and recharge.
>
> Loneliness instead is the word for melancholy, painful aloneness that generates anguish, anxiety and anger.
>
> Often being alone is the basis for creativity and innovation;
> the latter form accentuates the separation between yourself and others; "good" aloneness is the basis for leadership.
>
> (William Deresiewicz, www.theamericanscholar.org)

In terms of alliances, a leader must be **INCLUSIVE**, and this is why they must be able to attract and metabolize other people's ideas and values, not to feed their own interests, but to set up an alliance made of objectives and values: ethics, passion, empathy, work hard, play hard, sacrifice. Another discriminating factor is time – the relationship with the leader should come across as long-lasting/forever: a leader is never evasive or fleeting – we know that in the contemporary world we are all temporary, life itself is, but it is also true that people change jobs far more frequently now than they did 50 years ago. So the words "long-lasting" or "stable" might sound like oxymorons: the leader must be able to change job or position, and this is all part of the market, but at that precise moment when we encounter them, we must be able to perceive a stable contribution – one that is always present! And they are there to be a guide and pursue a shared objective. They are there to win together with the team.

KNOWING WHAT COUNTS FOR OTHERS

A leader must be able to understand what the objectives and values of the various stakeholders are: what really counts towards making their vision come true, but also what counts for the stakeholder and what counts for the team. Not everyone is motivated by money, or responsibility, or challenge. So leadership must be able to decline behavior and make changes according to the objective to be pursued. It's clear that if you want to change someone in the team, you will have to be ruthless. If instead you want to cultivate someone's talent, the leader has to be a **TALENT GARDENER**.

Jack Welch, president and CEO of General Electric, one of the greatest managers of the eighties, in his book *Winning*, repeated over and over again, like a mantra, the fact that 80% of a CEO's job is a matter of HR – or management of human resources – the scope of which is pretty wide-ranging: from talent scouting to placing the right people in the right places in the organization.

In the normal evolution of a company, the leader selects. Just like the trainer of a football team who must establish – for every single game – who is going to play and who, instead, will be on the sidelines; in the same way, at the end of the championship, someone will be sold and someone else bought on the market.

In his book *Leading: My Life*, Sir Alex Ferguson, trainer of Manchester United, spoke of leadership by starting out from the relationship that exists between athletes and trainers. In fact, in order to obtain the best results, managing a team means establishing who goes out onto the field: a trainer will place his trust in a captain who will coordinate the players during the match. In the same way, this *lean and flat* organizational pyramid is a concept that a leader must personally adopt: **DURING A MATCH, I MAY RUN LIKE HELL, BUT IF ALL THE PLAYERS AREN'T RUNNING, THEN THE TEAM WILL MOVE AS FAST OR AS SLOWLY AS THE SLOWEST PLAYER.**

KEEPING A TEAM UNITED

As in Sparta, where *agōgē* was applied,

> a strict educational re´gime and training based on discipline and obedience, to which every citizen of Sparta was subject, including the two royal dynasties (the Agiads and Eurypontids), from the age of 7 upwards. It entailed separation from the family, fostering loyalty to the group, military training and practice, hunting, dancing and preparation for social and civic life.

(Wikipedia, n.d.)

If need be, you must be able to fight in the shadows. A leader must be able to think on their feet.

They don't have all that much time to take decisions.

When they give an "order", it must be shared by the team to the extent that it is internalized by every team member (this is what happens in competitive sport when the drill is handed down by a master who leads the practice).

"You fall seven times, you get up eight."

This is a Japanese saying that lends itself to a subtle interpretation. You get up eight times if you fall seven. The first time you don't fall: you are born. True strength lies in getting back on your feet again. The idea is to go back and get fit again when there's a shared vision, and the whole team is fully committed to reaching these objectives, and where heart and courage will always be needed. And again, "There is only one conclusion to every story. We all fall down," says Keira Knightley, star of Tony Scott's film *Domino*. No one is perfect.

The only thing to do after making a mistake is *to get back onto your feet again.*

You get up again if you have **A VISION**, an intuition, an idea, a dream. If you have the ability, the training, the method, the muscle and the bones to allow you to get back up again. You get back up again if you have the heart and the grounding. And values that sustain the idea you want to put into practice: the alliances, an understanding of what **THE GOOD OF OTHERS** consists in.

The real secret of someone who wants to be a leader lies in the humble awareness that they are not perfect. You may not be a leader right from the start – and anyway who says you're one – and doubting, even doubting yourself, is fundamental; for some it may be a gift of the chromosomes, for others again the leader must be able to give proof of sensitivity. A leader mustn't be reckless but **COURAGEOUS**: must be aware of their own limits, including human ones. It's the leader who knows doubt and imperfection and is able to work selflessly for the satisfaction of pursuing a dream and an objective.

It isn't only the "classic" Sergio Marchionnes or Jack Welches who are leaders, Mother Teresa of Calcutta was a leader, too: that is, **THOSE WHO PURSUE A VISION AND WHOSE WHOLE LIFE IS PERMEATED BY THIS VISION**, enriching every aspect of it, and giving others a practical example through their own trajectory.

A leader has **HUMANITY**. Some say, instead, that a "hardliner" is better, a severe leader, but this is not the model we propose in this approach.

The leader is grateful and is always asking themselves:

Why me?
Understanding the Mistake
There are big mistakes and little mistakes.

Statistically, big mistakes are made less frequently, but they do occur and certainly weigh heavily. When is a big mistake made, and what is it? These are the times, for example, when you adopt solutions and then realize you were wrong because perhaps you didn't take into account **EXTERNAL FACTORS**, reasons independent of yourself; at other times, instead, the big mistakes may relate to **PEOPLE OR SITUATIONS YOU COME ACROSS**, and in any case these sorts of mistakes are all due to a common denominator: you don't believe strongly enough in your path and your vision, so you change your route. Because you start to be afraid you aren't capable of facing the forest or getting through to the end of the labyrinth. Someone or something creates these thoughts in you – a genesis you had nothing to do with – and it's then that you make your biggest mistake of all: giving up your dream.

Every time I'm in difficulty, I remember two things:

The first is the exhortation inscribed above the gateway to the temple of Apollo in Delphi

gnōthi seautón – know yourself

I use this at times when it's useful for me to go back over my own tracks. And then. When I don't have enough faith in my ideas:

I've learned to **LIST THE THINGS I'VE DONE WELL IN THE COURSE OF TIME**. From the beginning up to the moment I find myself making the decision (difficult of course, which puts me in a difficult situation). I write down everything in chronological order. This allows me to get myself into focus, to immediately see, as though on a master plan, the **OVERALL PROJECTION** of my path.

Lastly, a leader must always remember

never to betray their own self.

Little mistakes, on the other hand, are made every day and mostly regard **TACTICAL DECISIONS**: in absolute terms, we know that a leader should direct their choices towards what is good, rather than towards the best, the *optimum*, and yet, mistakes are made daily all the same.

Why towards what is good and not towards the best, we might wonder. This might seem absurd for a leader and a visionary. Instead, there is a rationale to it.

BECAUSE IN THE TIME TAKEN TO ACT THE BEST WAY POSSIBLE OR TAKE THE BEST DECISION POSSIBLE, A LOT CAN BE DONE WELL. And the sum total of those "wells" may be infinitely superior to a single "best". For theoreticians of *Gestalt* (the psychology of form and shape: a movement that developed in Berlin at the start of the twentieth century in opposition to structuralism): "The whole is more than the sum of its single parts", and this means that our total perception does not depend solely on the sum of individual sensorial impulses but on that extra *quid* that allows us to grasp the form as a whole. The sum is greater than its individual parts: this is so in the case of a beautiful melody played by an orchestra.

The important thing – and this goes both for managerial choices and for life choices – is that once you have understood that you've made a mistake, you shouldn't be afraid to change, you must not insist on your mistake (just out of an inner severity that leads to you refusing to see the evidence – what would otherwise be crystal clear to you – or perhaps because you can't bring yourself to overcome a prejudice). Being a leader also means having the ability to admit your mistakes and say, "I was wrong."

EXTRA 1: *WHAT IF*: IF THE COMPANY WERE A SPORT

Leadership is a team sport. What are the rules of engagement?

There's a president who finances the team. A trainer who decides how to play, how to train, what schemes to adopt – is it best to go for attack or zone defense, mark your man, keep possession of the ball, rely on a fast game? In all cases, it's a sport where all the players must give their best. Not necessarily in football or volleyball, basketball or water polo. It's a competitive team sport in which a collective victory is obtained thanks to individuals, as happens in tennis, in the Davis Cup. There is a selector, there's a federation. Every day you train and you improve. And then on the day of the competition, you're on your own. You try to win in the interests of the whole team.

Elements of competition for leadership:

- a strict training schedule [it must be tough and intense];
- sacrifice.

But

I want my top players to know that the attitude for engaging battle is always:

- when we're on the field, you're free!

I WANT INDIVIDUAL TALENTS TO BE ABLE TO GIVE REIN TO THEIR IMAGINATION, WHILST REMEMBERING THAT YOU NEVER PLAY FOR YOURSELF ALONE BUT ALWAYS AS A TEAM

I like to talk to people, and I try to be there for everyone. And I am a trainer who takes responsibility for the team: when we play badly and the results are negative; when we win, I think it's right to acknowledge the merits of my team. The trainer, the leader, must protect and bring out the best, be able to enjoy and to celebrate the great moments. **YOU NEVER LET GO, BUT IT'S ESSENTIAL FOR EVERYONE TO GIVE THEIR UTMOST. I CAN'T BE CONTENT WITH PLAYERS WHO JUST DO THEIR HOMEWORK.** It's important, instead, for everyone to want to express themselves to the limit, through – and with – the team: with heart and soul and with their passion.

EXTRA 2: THE ENVIRONMENT AS AN ASSET IN THE PRESENT – FUTURE

The environment is and always will be an essential issue for every company. There is no administrator, no leader, who can afford not to consider sustainability, green priorities, or the concept of a circular economy essential to her/his own company. Environmental issues are to do both with civil conscience and with marketing and communication. There is and always will be discussion of the relationship between humankind and the planet Earth, and from a certain point of view, these are **REWARDING THEMES**. Companies work on profits and the green market will become increasingly important worldwide.

A leader who deals with the development of products for the end consumer, and with sourcing, and thus of services and production, must necessarily direct her/his strategy in this sense, at the level of communication, too.

Everything must be low on pollution, with an impact as close to zero as possible. The public and customers all demand this, and it is also a matter of ethics. We are human beings on a vast planet. We're part of a balance that has held for millions of years. We live, they say, in the Anthropocene era, that of climate change. A leader must have knowledge and awareness, form their own ideas within the vaster balance of the world, so as to introduce their vision (as an enterprise) in relation to a world that is continually changing and consists of economy and relations, rationality and emotions, the value of what we eat, the soil on which we grow the vines that produce our wines.

> GDP measures neither our wit nor our courage,
> neither our wisdom nor our learning,
> neither our compassion nor our devotion to our country,
> it measures everything in short, except that which makes life
> worthwhile.
>
> **ROBERT "BOB" KENNEDY (1925–1968)**

I love the sea.

Not by chance my favorite color is blue.

For me blue immediately conjures up the endless skies of the American plains.

At the same time I love the mountains both in summer and in winter. I love the change in the air brought about by the altitude – seeing things from up high – the horizon of nature, relations with the trees, mountains, animals, allowing the mind to detach (and rest) from our daily environment, in the cities.

To walk along the beach in the early morning. The dawn, the sun rising in a cloudless sky.

These aren't just signs of a fine-weather day. They are part of the **GEOGRAPHY OF DAYS** that form us. They are even pertinent to something highly useful, that will accompany us in all our relations, human and economic, and define our **INNER CLIMATE**.

Grounding | Leonidas

It is 480 BC when King Leonidas I of Sparta starts out on his march with his Lacedaemonian warriors towards Thermopylae.

The god-emperor Xerxes, at the head of the most variegated army history had ever known, is about to come onto the scene. Elephants, enormous ships, black assassins with their faces masked. But Xerxes' army will find the *300* facing it.

In that battle the 300 will perish, and yet their sacrifice will allow first Athens and then the whole of Greece to defeat the invaders' attack.

Where does it come from, this devotion on which Leonidas' character is grounded? Way back in time.

The initiation of Leonidas, "son of the lion", took place, as for all the young warriors and healthy sons of Sparta, in the forest. During that *agóghe´* at the age of 8, Leonidas was left alone to survive in the woods, where he faced the cold, lack of food, solitude, and finally the wolf: he knew he had to defeat it or he would perish, torn apart by its fangs.

"More than forty years have passed since the episode with the wolf in that ice-cold winter. Now, as then, it is not fear that has the upper hand. No. it is restlessness, a more acute perception of things. The rocks beneath his feet, the salt breeze. The snoring and the breathing of the three hundred lads entrusted to him . . . All ready to die for him without hesitation, right down to the last man."

Being educated to be solid, it is the freedom that comes from cast-iron discipline that allows Leonidas to govern wisely and firmly, with a ferocious, controlled anger, unscrupulously, at times even crazily. According to the historian Plutarch, when Xerxes demanded that Leonidas and the Greeks lay down their arms, the king of Sparta replied, "*Molòn labé*," literally "Come and get them."

> **The great difference between Leonidas' 300 – as for Jasons' 50 Argonauts, and other Greeks – was this very awareness: the idea of freedom, the land, their loved ones, the fields of wheat to protect from the iron and the metal. This is what gives a leader the strength to do what he believes is right, until the end.**

KEY TAKEAWAYS

"Our" leader

- has a solid grounding (love, loyalty, inclusivity, team management);
- can fight in the shadows and, if he falls, can always get up onto their feet again;
- never betrays their own self and is not afraid of changing;
- never "gives up";
- is aware there is no planet b.

CHAPTER 7
State of lead

DOI: 10.4324/9781003378532-10

Strong with the strong, equal with the team.

Leadership has a positive concept of alliance, vision, ability to protect the team. It's essential to be perceived as **ONE OF US**, someone who can protect and tries to obtain the best from everyone. I don't believe that the best is obtained by a show of strength, arrogance, or terror, and even if there are many leaders of this type, this is not what I would define as positive leadership.

Instead, I believe in a concept of positive leadership able to make the team into a united group. And how is this done? By going forwards together. I don't like generals who do battle by standing back and watching, sending their troops on ahead. A leader is **BRAVEHEART**, the untamed spirit of the Scots. You are at the front. You are with your people.

The correct approach of a leader is also evident in another attitude. **BEING STRONG WITH THE STRONG** means being able to defend your ideas and visions with courage and strength. Even towards people in a position of greater, or equal, responsibility or power. **ARROGANCE MEANS THINKING YOU ARE SUPERIOR.** More often than not this will mean assuming a position in an unduly obtuse manner. Those who are strong in their own ideas are instead convinced, courageous, and can argue their choices. A leader is a real person and may also be afraid.

In a sense, what we are saying here might seem strange and contrary to the "Leonidas model", whilst in reality it is quite coherent. Leonidas, too, was afraid, I believe, and it's the very awareness of this fear, the awareness of it being possible to lose, of not knowing what's going to happen, that stops you from not fearing any outcome.

"I've faced many battles," comments Mario Draghi at the question, "What makes you think you can make it?" And his reply is, "Because I've quite often made it." This is what a leader is like: they have often made it. For a leader every challenge is a new one, and they start anew every time.

There are people who are born with a strong awareness of their means and their strength. These are the people who might be defined natural leaders and express this tendency from a very young age. Others, instead, take longer. For myself, for instance, as for others, the **AWARENESS OF LEADERSHIP** built up through a few successes and defeats, after having been afraid and faced the fear, with the reasonable certainty that sooner or later the obstacles would be overcome.

You get over initial difficulties, a few mistakes, but "I've quite often made it," and the more often this happens, the more your awareness increases. Leadership is a path that never comes to an end, except for the enlightened, but that is a different matter. At times, however, the enlightened risk their leadership becoming reckless and unscrupulous, to the extent that being too sure of your own capacities leads to lack of fear. Fear, instead, is a great asset. You mustn't stop, impede, or block; in fact, I believe that the "right" level of anxiety means acquiring awareness of the fact that every decision you take impacts on the lives of others, on your own, and on the world around you.

One of the most important features of leadership is responsibility. Self-esteem and confidence also increase at every obstacle overcome, as well as mental fitness. The confidence that you can have a go and commit yourself. The final result, however, will depend on how firmly united the team is, and there is also a good measure of luck in "succeeding": a series of (macrocosmic) events you are not in control of. All the same, in the end what makes you who you are will be a sum that is greater than the individual parts.

The courage to be/live and fight.

A real leader isn't arrogant and doesn't think they know everything or that they are (or can become) God. They believe they are an explorer. A real leader has intuition, vision, and knows that the world is full of obstacles but recognizes them and it's then that they forge ahead. They are an explorer, sees the general picture, and is less interested in the waystages because they are on a path. Their own. They have dynamic objectives and are coherent with those objectives. **A LEADER IS A DIRECTION.** As an explorer, they never abandon their mission. They move forward. Obviously with their own experience. Which in this case is technical experience and knowledge, of the team, of relations and relationships.

Where leadership is concerned, there is an issue of **CONTINUITY**. There are leaders who become one with their idea and with the enterprise. Who stay with a company for 20 years, for example. But there are also leaders who change position and company every two years. As in everything, a single, absolute truth does not exist. There is an advantage in knowing every single aspect, every nook and cranny of a company, and there are advantages in getting to know a number of different situations. It all depends on your trajectory and on the type of leadership needed. If new paths are to be opened up, then someone with more varied experience will be "worth" more. If, instead, a state of affairs must be maintained, then a stable leader is more useful.

The theme of exploration in leadership has to do with a long-term vision, and later, when one has been achieved, there will be another. When you see that you no longer have a long-term vision, then perhaps your time is up.

I seek challenges:

- I want freedom to express myself.
- I want to be able to construct, to build.
- I am a person who builds bridges that lead to winning new territories. And when you get there, you build a city, and when that city has been built, you build another, leaving the inhabitants to run it.

I am interested in paths that are stimulating and at the same time require commitment: you stop, you put down foundations, **YOU MUST BE ABLE TO ATTRACT** prospective inhabitants of the place, who only exist in your brain up to then, as an inner habitat. You must create a place where it's good to live: not until you have created it will you be able to move somewhere else. My dream is to see the whole world.

I don't know if I'll manage this in a single lifetime. But I do know I want to be a free, world citizen and that I want to think and do things – in my own small way – that others have never done. This is basically what drives me.

IF THE LEADER WERE A SYMBOL there would be a lion on their supercostume. The lion is courageous, like Richard the Lionheart. The lion is strong, knows how to fight and can be ferocious, because its values are linked to family and the defense of its cubs, the pack, and its offspring. If I were to look to the animal world, I would choose a feline – whether lion, black panther, or leopard – this image gives me a lot of strength and a vision. As a symbol, I would also choose the Sun.

IF THEY WERE A SUPERHERO, WHAT SUPERPOWER WOULD A LEADER HAVE?

The courage to tackle any situation without fear.

One example.

The strength of Black Panther, whether in the film or the comic, can defeat the prejudice of presumed racial superiority. In fact, there, Wakanda, a state somewhere in the heart of Africa, is discovered to be highly advanced technologically. Overturning, in one fell swoop, the myth of "the white man" and centuries of racism.

It's always prejudice that stops us from understanding. The stupidity of applied racism, which believes that leadership is tied to skin color or to height, to the fact of being white with blue eyes or having a crooked nose. It's the inability to overcome prejudices, which, instead of creating, gives rise to divisions and boundaries we can't escape from. But a leader moves beyond that. Not only do they manage to get out of the labyrinth. They are already standing above it and can therefore see things from above. It's their own vision.

OUR BODY SPEAKS

The way we walk, eat, whether we've suffered traumas, our eyes, the melancholy of a life lived more or less dangerously, whether we're getting separated, or have lost our mother, whether, instead, a child has been born, all this becomes part of our way of relating to the world.

I carry with me, for example, an ancient Celtic blessing in Gaelic – the language spoken in Scotland and Ireland. It's what I would like to wish everyone, and it goes as follows:

> May the road rise to meet you.
> May the wind be always at your back,
> May the sun shine warm upon your face and the rain fall soft upon your fields.
>
> And until we meet again,
> May God hold you in the hollow of his hand.

It's a splendid wish because it refers to the future (the journey).
To speed (the wind) and to the importance for each of us to reach **objectives**.
The sun is the theme of serenity, living life as we encounter the path.
The wind signifies never forgetting the here and now, both in life and in managerial choices.

The rain falling on your fields: you don't have it in your power to command rainfall; it's the moves you make that help you. Your fields grow dry if you don't have a team or a vision, but also if you don't have Luck on your side, the fickle goddess without whom no rain will suffice and no crops will flourish.

The palm is the final wish, because if God – whoever *the* god in question is – is holding you in his hand, your decisions will almost always be "right". The decisions are right if they are taken wholeheartedly, with humanity and the awareness of making choices guided by data but inspired by the need to imagine new paths not yet travelled. In leadership there is an element that is almost divine, supernatural: intuition.

So we must read what we have said, reread the words we pronounced to build the project that we have in mind, and make sure that those who work with us have them engraved in their mind and completely absorbed them. First and foremost, we ourselves.

IF THE LEADER WERE A SUPERHERO, WHAT WOULD THEIR "CITY" BE?

The ideal place for practicing leadership as I understand it is Sydney. A wonderful city with all the features of a metropolis but surrounded by spectacular natural beauty.

The **SEA-OCEAN** at Bondi Bay.

bondi

/bo'n-d[a]i/ Aboriginal term meaning "water breaking against the rock" or "sound of the water breaking on the rocks".

Marvelous beaches that make Sydney quite different from any other metropolis in the world. And all around, the boundless Australian bush. Today's global world is a huge metropolis. A world in which we are all extremely close. In Sydney you have access to all the comforts of modern life: culture and sport, but only a step away the possibility of enjoying unspoiled nature, the marine world and the mountains.

At the same time, I realize I love Miami infinitely. I've lived there, and I think it's the best city. I would still like to be living there, if possible, of course, bringing it a bit closer to Italy. But Sydney remains top of the list if it's a matter of building a world that doesn't exist yet, giving substance to "the possibility of": there are big companies, the Australian banks. And . . .

Australia isn't a fake world; it achieves a good balance between modernity and the environment – and it doesn't do this "only" in the sense of sustainability (all too often a mask for green washing) but goes further: there it really is a question of learning to enjoy the beauty of all the Earth's various places.

We **ARE ONLY ON THIS PLANET FOR A HANDFUL OF YEARS** – too often we forget this, whilst instead we should remember it every day. Too often we forget how inspiring it can be to watch the dawn break, a sunset on the beach at the end of the day, sinking your bare feet into the cool sand in the evening after having worked all day. This is a theme for those who want to practice leadership today.

If I were a superhero and had to build my personal Wakanda, it would be a New York with Miami's beaches or the sea of the Maldives, and this beach would, of course, be run by beach guards from Emilia-Romagna, whilst in the background there would be the marvelous mountains of our Alps, with professionally managed ski lifts and the culture of hospitality of the great resorts of Aspen, or Salt Lake City. If cities like this could be built, they'd become centers of super business(!).

*After work, going down to the beach,
sinking your bare feet into the cool sand
in the evening.*

State of lead | Mario Draghi
Economist

We know that Mario Draghi is a basketball fan and a supporter of the Roman team.

The expression of a real "third" leadership which can be strong with the strong and at the same time is able to safeguard the interests of the various stakeholders.

Right after the famous words "Whatever it takes", pronounced during an investors' forum in London in the middle of the first drastic economic crisis to hit Europe, the then president of the ECB, Draghi, said that the institute would, in fact, do "everything necessary", to save the euro. Born in Rome in 1947, he is the son of a banker and a pharmacist.

After graduating at the Sapienza University with Federico Caffe', he first entered the Massachusetts Institute of Technology (MIT) and then, amongst other universities, taught at the Ca' Foscari in Venice, later joining the Board of Trustees of Princeton University.

His career has been studded with high-profile international experiences which have "built" him into an eminently practical and pragmatic figure, forged by great experience both in the public and in the private sectors: CEO of the World Bank in Washington first, then minister of the treasury, vice chairman and managing director of Goldman Sachs Group, Inc., one of the largest investment banks in the world, subsequently governor of the Banca d'Italia, as well as president of the European Central Bank, right up to his latest position as prime minister of Italy in 2021.

The expression of an extremely credible and transparent leadership, Super Mario(!) is a leader who does what he says he will and says what he does. He is a man who has made sobriety and rigor his trademark – he lives in *buen retiro* in Umbria with his wife, who is an expert on English literature – a man with ethics, he has the great ability to be bipartisan, a much-appreciated expert both by the experts and by politics.

Unlike other contemporary leaders, who tend to be loud communicators, Mario Draghi embodies a long-term vision and is a leader with vertical competences, able to gather people together and guide them, coordinating the best of them by means of clear communication, which is assertive and nonviolent but at the same time convincing.

KEY TAKEAWAYS

"Our" leader

- is strong with the strong, equal with their team;
- can protect and tries to obtain the best from everyone;
- "has quite often made it";
- builds their leadership by means of a path that is never-ending;
- has the courage to face any situation without fear.

CHAPTER 8

Self-awareness

DOI: 10.4324/9781003378532-11

IDENTITY

Having a personal identity is necessary for every leader. A "person's" characteristics make their leadership specific. What is identity for a leader? It consists of their basic characteristics, style, recognizability, lifestyle, even *style* of dressing, smiling, or way of getting irritated – all aspects of the way they communicate, not only in words but also emotionally through body language. Identity is extremely important for a leader, just as brand identity is for a company. A leader has an identity when you can appreciate all its positive aspects, and at the same time, you also know their negative sides, the rough, and more jagged edges and therefore know who they are and what you can expect. This is what they are, and it is "authentic".

A leader is capable of guiding, knows what their bases are (ethics, **JUSTICE**, strength, freedom, **TEAM**, FITNESS, drive, **PASSION**, work hard, play hard, family), whatever they are, these are the elements that make up their identity. Some of these aspects come from DNA and are part of their habitat: where they were born, how they grew up, how they have reacted to life events. Others instead come from training and accumulated experience: these aspects can be partly modified, attenuated, made up for. They are collateral aspects.

A LEADER MUST BE/BE SEEN TO BE CONSISTENT OVER THE YEARS

We must be able to codify what sort of leader Sergio Marchionne is and at the same time know that his will be a completely different leadership to that of Michelle Obama, or Batman. It is always essential to ask ourselves what we can expect from "that" particular leader. From yourself, for example?

Then there is a leader identity that must filter down into the company and the brands you work with on each individual occasion. **A LEADER (ALSO) REPRESENTS A VISION OVER 5–6 YEARS.** The question is, will they be able to transfer it to the company, and in addition, are they a one-man band or a leader who plays in and with their team?

AFFINITY

This regards the creation of a team: a leader can create and must not (nor wants to) have clones alongside them; they prefer like-minded people, with whom they can share the same values. In the global environment (quite simply the world today changes far more quickly compared to the age of Sparta and the Battle of Thermopylae), a leader must be able to create and convey values and vehicle a basic, shared culture amongst the like-minded on the inside, as far as possible applying the criterion of diversity in forming the team so as to obtain a balance of thought, competences, age, and visions, knowing that in the end they will have to find a common denominator and take decisions. When lacking complete consensus, their position will be the decisive one.

THIS IS THE CONCEPT OF AFFINITY/DIVERSITY IN THE CREATION OF THE LEADER'S IDENTITY

A leader's affinity manifests itself when they create the "perfect alchemy", as when preparing a recipe: a dish can't consist of a single ingredient; there must be an amalgam. The same applies to people.

Affinity is horizontal/diversity is vertical.

It will be the grounding, character traits rather than a single specific competence that makes the difference – the Americans spoke of **melting**

pot, the French would speak of **METISSAGE** – so as to make the most of all the ingredients, all the visions in a correct constructive debate.

"Constructive", this is the right word: because what you intend to do is

Build the future.

Invitation to supper with the leader.

Double first course according to tradition:

Tortellini in brodo
Tagliatella al ragù

Two great dishes that explore the concept of pasta and at the same time are protein-based. In July, as at the change of season in the fall, complete dishes in the Italian tradition, simple to prepare and therefore essential. The substance of the genuine dishes of the past: authentic madeleines of taste, the quality of the pasta, of the ragù with the tagliatelle and the filling of the tortellini, the rough volume, and the paper-thin pasta make these foods unique.

Demonstrating that simplicity can rise to exceptional levels which no complicated dish can ever attain.

Grilled meat and locally sourced vegetables (0 km)

Organically farmed meat (animals raised in the open air without the use of antibiotics). Selected ingredients, light dishes, a barbecue coal grill in the Appenines, simple cooking, top-quality meat and vegetables, few sauces to detract from the taste of genuine, local meat.

Fruit of the Season

Dessert

Chocolate mousse: chocolate stimulates endorphins
and the production of serotonin; a sugar-free sweet and a
healthy one that makes for well-being.

Wine list
Welcome cocktail of your choice
Italian Franciacorta, French champagne, Spanish El cava

First course
Italian red wine (Tuscan or Veneto)
Côtes du Rhône
Californian Merlot

Second course
Barolo or Châteauneuf-du-Pape
or Californian Cabernet Sauvignon

Dessert wines Passito
di Pantelleria
Sauternes
Austrian-German Eiswein
Family Nocino

KNOW YOUR OWN LIMITS

We are a geography. There are mental borders and, at the same time, physical borders. Indeed, *mens sana in corpore sano* went the famous Latin saying, taken from the opening lines of Juvenal's *Satires*. Knowing the geography of your body reminds you who you are. Every time I think about the 44 stitches in my forehead, I remember that in 1994 I was a lad of just 28. I was in the United States when they told me I had a little problem to solve. I remember facing the operation with the utmost psychological and physical attention.

TRAUMAS AND ADVERSITIES HAVE TWOFOLD POWER. At the beginning you have to accept the situation and understand how to get over it, whatever happens. Once you've faced it, however things go, you'll have obtained a victory: whether the outcome of a battle is negative or positive, you will in any case have acquired the certainty of engagement, and you'll have put yourself to the test. This experience will fortify you; even more, it will be imprinted in your mental DNA. It will constitute and become a way of thinking/seeing the world/acting.

This behavior will subsequently filter down, in turn, into

- all the things you do;
- whoever comes into contact with you.

Years later you don't notice the scar any longer, but when you do see the scars marking your body, you remember **what** you faced, **who** stood alongside you. "You see" the good moments, the . . . ones that weren't so good. Going back in my memory, I realize that experiences, the negative included, give you much more than they take away.

I think of another part of my body: my knee, where a ligament is now missing and which causes little outbreaks of arthritis now and then. But I think of it with endless love, mostly because that scar reminds me of a splendid period in my life: the years when I played squash and managed to make the Italian team in the European and World Championships, thanks to that knee which is now injured. On how many other occasions do we remember what we did thanks to an injury or a scar that's still there; it's true, we hurt ourselves, but it is also a **SYMBOL OF HOW MUCH WE RISKED AND LIVED OUR LIFE**.

Every injury recalls a story of growth. From an individual story, a general lesson can be extracted. Taking part in competitive sport teaches you to compete and fight and in addition brings some absolute values with it: the importance of training, constancy, getting used to the idea that you may lose, and that you must always commit to the utmost all the same.

I don't belong to the Pierre de Coubertin school – the important thing is to participate – but instead I'm for a reworking of his motto, that is: **"THE IMPORTANT THING IS TO BE ABLE TO COMPETE, ENJOY YOURSELF AND, IF POSSIBLE, WIN."** Because if you have the talent and the physical ability to win, it's a pity not to.

DOES MY BODY REPRESENT ME?

> The conditional is a verb form used mostly to indicate an event or
> situation that only occurs if a determined condition is satisfied.
>
> (Wikipedia, 2023)

I would like to be 1.90 m and weigh 78 kg, all muscle if possible.

Instead, I "inhabit" an average build. And yet I always have to ask myself:
can this be a problem? Or should I, instead, reckon simply with what
I have? In any case I shall never live up to my expectations. Instead, I shall
play my game according to my strong and weak points. You must always
consider what you're capable of doing.

On the basis of your own resources, where can you get to?

Barack Obama, for example, managed to become leader of one of the most important world powers: the United States of America. The first *black* president in history! Elected for two terms of office. He got beyond the barriers of racism, even his own and those of his adversaries. How? Simply by being himself, to the highest degree. This is one of the greatest lessons for anyone who wants to be a leader.

A leader must be aware and must study to get ideas

Self-awareness | Lisa Su
Manager

For *Forbes*, Lisa Su was one of the top self-made women in 2020. She is president of AMD, Advanced Micro Devices, a Canadian company producing semiconductors, driver of one of the greatest recent innovations in the sector of technology.

Since she became CEO in 2014, AMD's shares have risen over 20 times, with a market capitalization of 100 billion dollars.

Born in Taiwan in 1969, Lisa Tzwu-Fang Su moved to the United States with her family at the age of 3: "I just had this great curiosity to see how things worked", the passion for taking the world apart, and rebuilding it according to her own personal language.

From the Chinese *hakka* to American English, Su's first lexicon was formed at the Bronx High School of Science in New York City and perfected at the prestigious MIT (Massachusetts Institute of Technology) where she graduated in electrical engineering with a doctor's thesis titled "Extreme-submicrometer silicon-on-isolator (SOI)-MOSFETs".

In 2002 she was mentioned as one of the Top 100 Young Innovators by the *MIT Technology Review*.

At their first work experience, everyone gives their utmost. You speak the language you know. You use your strong points. The awareness of your own resources.

As a member of the technical staff at Texas Instruments, Lisa Su therefore applied what she had learned as a little girl – from taking apart her brother's remote-controlled automobiles to find out what was inside them; she did the same when she was taken on as vice president of IMB's R&D center in the semiconductor division: "My specialization wasn't copper, but I moved where the problems were."

Never step back, pliancy (which is, by the way, one of the main properties of semiconductors), Su is the epitome of the operational leader: for a year she held the position of technical assistant for Louis V. Gerstner Jr., president and CEO of the "Big Blue" IBM until 2002, from whom she inherited one of Gerstner's favorite sayings: "What I learnt from IBM is that the culture is everything."

A leader must be aware and must study to get ideas. Like Su, who in 2015 realized the need to broaden AMD's market and signed agreements with PlayStation Sony and Xbox One, to integrate the processors in their video game consoles. Before she came along, AMD's non-PC market was worth 10%; after Lisa Su and her team's vision of development, it was 40%.

KEY TAKEAWAYS

"Our" leader

- has their own identity and it is the authentic one;
- looks for the right mix of affinity and diversity in building their team;
- doesn't want clones alongside themselves but prefers **like-minded** people with whom the same values can be shared;
- is capable of enjoying the goods things in life (a good supper);
- wants to compete, enjoy themselves, and if possible, win;
- is "curious to know how things work".

80/20

CHAPTER 9
Doing

DOI: 10.4324/9781003378532-12

THE RULE OF 80/20

Pareto's Principle is taught in big consultancy agencies and is one of the tools a manager uses when they have to take decisions – rapidly. It would be great to have time to analyze all the problems that come up. But the best is the enemy of what's good, says the rule of 80/20, and time is a limited resource. The 80/20 rule means concentrating on that 20% of topics that can yield 80% of the answers, focusing the analyses possible at that precise moment on these topics.

WITH 20% OF THE EFFORT, YOU OBTAIN 80% OF THE ANSWERS

It's not always enough, but it must suffice to choose a direction and make a working hypothesis. Start out along a path. Then you must increase your time – work analysis and figure out what it means in terms of **QUALITY** because that 80% of answers represents the clearest feedback, the logical and immediate consequences. To these, more must necessarily be added.

Meanwhile, however, thanks to this information, you'll be able to get on with your task; if things weren't like this, young managers/young leaders, most of all, might get lost in the meanders of infinite analyses, thus losing sight of the most important thing: the big picture, the vision of **WHERE YOU WANT TO GET TO**. The "80/20" rule is therefore necessary to make a start on managerial culture. It's the first step in dealing with the problem: it delimits, helps you understand, teaches you to choose the relevant themes, and put other layers of analyses into better focus. It's not the only or the ultimate answer for approaching the solution. As the Americans say:

AFTER HAVING MADE A HYPOTHESIS ON AN 80/20 BASIS, THEN YOU HAVE TO PEEL THE ONION

Peeling the onion means solving one thing at a time, just as you peel off the various layers of the plant. Or delving back into time, we might remember the words of *Doctor Subtilis* Duns Scoto, the thirteenth-century philosopher:

Ex falso sequitur libet

which doesn't necessarily mean

Those who start out well finish well

It's quite possible, on the other hand, that starting out "well" offers a better probability of **FINISHING WELL**. In the same way, though, something may start out badly and be corrected *in itinere*. Or again, we might start out well, become enamored of an idea, a project, commit time and resources to it, and in the end all the same – since we live in a constantly changing world – not obtain the result we hoped for. So we might re-elaborate the concept as

Those who start out well are halfway to the end of their work. There exists a causal link that can translate into competitive edge.

Let's move on
Let's make it happen
Let's make a deal

This is an attitude – three ways of expressing the best of the American culture of doing.

1. Let's move on

Means: "let's go forward, not stop before an obstacle". If you can't get over a wall or if there's an unsolved dilemma, the important thing is not to give in to the logic of stopping. But to press on, then perhaps you can go back, make a U-turn.

According to US thinking, you mustn't stop short at determined things. At the most if you're doing a deal, you have to find an agreement: this is the culture of doing that is the subject of the famous international bestseller *Getting to Yes: Negotiating an Agreement without Giving In* (over 8 million copies sold all over the world) by Fisher and Ury.

ROGER FISHER is a professor emeritus, director of the Harvard Negotiation Project, and founder of two consultancy organizations devoted to strategic consultancy and negotiation training. **WILLIAM URY** is a world-renowned specialist in negotiation and a distinguished senior fellow of Harvard Law School's Program on Negotiation. Author of *The Power of a Positive No.*

The book is based on three premises:

- **DON'T BARGAIN OVER POSITIONS**
- **SEPARATE THE PEOPLE FROM THE PROBLEM**
- **INSIST ON OBJECTIVE CRITERIA**

2. Let's make it happen

A common path must be found. In leadership there mustn't be a winner and a loser: the result must be an advantage/useful/fruitful to both parties.

3. Let's make a deal

Let's come to an agreement, in terms of a **PACT**. Here, the Anglo-Saxon cultures teach us something basic to business: precisely by virtue of the fact that that they are not grossly self-referential or individualistic to the extreme, they prove instead to be utilitarian and pragmatic "**WE CULTURES**".

It's not
I Move On
or
You Move On
it's

Let's move on *together.*

"I'm offering you something" is a concise and inclusive **FORMULA OF CONCESSION**. In business it's a premise that interprets the culture of doing things together in a positive sense. The deal can't be a bargain for one of the parties only. It may be on one occasion, and if it is, then the *gentlemen's agreement* implies that next time the deal will go to the other side, to the side that's had to "succumb". Like this, everyone will find it in their interests to extend the agreement.

In this game there is no information asymmetry.

MAKE IT HAPPEN!

Once the pact has been made, there can be no second thoughts, no "going back": personal credibility is at stake, the leader's word, and (also) future business. This is part of what remains **UNSAID**, which at times is more important than written or formal agreements because it's based on mutual trust. You're making a commitment with the other side: "let's get over the resistance." This is where the etymological root of the term "rival" comes into play, understood as *rivus*, that is, the one who, in that precise moment, simply finds themself on the other side of the river. Once the path has been established together, however, together with all that is to be done and having checked every aspect, rather than exhausting yourself in an embarrassing come-and-go, you take heart and take a running jump over the obstacle:

And now, let's go!
Let's do something.

In this way, from an interesting level of discussion, you establish – by mutual agreement – where you're going, what objectives are to be reached (in the short, medium, and long term), what **IMPLEMENTATION** is necessary, right up to the actual **ACTION** or **WHAT WE HAVE DO TO MAKE THE THING HAPPEN.** In the meantime, take action; then, if needs be:

- correct;
- recognize your mistakes;
- change your mind;
- be capable of self-criticism;
- discover your errors.

This is a logic I learned from one of history's most incredible leaders in the world of sport:

> I must have shot 11 winners right before the whistle, and another 17 times at least at 10 seconds to the end, but in my career I missed over 9,000 shots. I lost almost 300 games. 36 times my team mates trusted me with the decisive shot . . . and I missed. I missed many, many, many times in my life. And that's why in the end I won them all.
>
> (Michael Jeffrey Jordan, US basketball player, 1963)

The words of *Air Jordan*, in 1999 voted "the greatest North-American athlete of the twentieth century" by the TV sports channel ESPN – mean, for everyone, without exception (and without apology):

You gonna make it.

It's a message of great hope and, at the same time, of responsibility assumed because he – *His Airness* – is talking directly to you and looking you straight in the eyes. He says:

Whatever talent you have, if you don't give it a try, you're wasting a divine gift.

Jordan is obviously a wonder of the universe, an athlete who defies the law of physics. At the Slam Dunk Contest in 1988 he made a leap over two meters long, attaining a height of over 3.05 meters and slammed the ball into the basket with his legs wide open (a feat of athletics that put the logo on the gym shoes dedicated to him by the mythical Nike brand).

But first and foremost, before becoming a champion, MJ gave it a try. He made all the necessary sacrifices to get there. He led a sporting life, with all its merits but, at the same time, assuming the responsibilities this implied. The question, therefore, is

Have you "really" given it a try?

Because a lot of people don't actually give it a try, only to complain afterwards **BECAUSE THEY DIDN'T**. But you. Have you put your image, your heart, your pride on the line? From this perspective, MJ's message becomes extremely positive. You can only win if you give it a try. **HERE, THE LESSON IS HOW TO LEARN FROM YOUR MISTAKES.** Jordan's story is one of stamina.

Jordan represents the leader who makes a mistake once and then works not to make others, continuing to commit more and more intensely. He represents the need to have a vision and know how to change it if necessary. This is an essential characteristic for trainers, too, who change schemes during a game. And change players only a few minutes before the whistle, because they think that perhaps a certain player will be decisive in that particular game. It's an inspiration. An idea. And perhaps it works!

The same happens when managers are obliged to change certain key figures in the organigram, figures they may have affection for but who are not performing. Or when there are directions they've been concentrating on but then comes the realization they're not working: the foreign market, for example, or a market that suddenly implodes. You must be able to go back again.

A LEADER DECIDES TODAY ABOUT TODAY, WITHIN A VISION THAT LOOKS TO TOMORROW

You have to improve the strong points and at the same time not be afraid of the weak ones, the ones you have to work on and, if needs be, get help with: it is here that the **winning team intervenes**.

A leader is the trainer of their team; to extend the metaphor of the football trainer: if I have a strong player on the right wing but a weak one on the left, I won't make him play with his left foot only. I certainly don't want him to forget that foot, but I don't want him to suffer the stress of improving it more than the one he uses naturally; in fact, my task will be to develop that **natural predisposition**, his right foot; that's the one I want to make him excel with. So a "true" leader wants to bring out the best in everyone; paraphrasing the great Leonardo Sciascia: "Each to their own."

THE K FACTOR

Apart from a few cases, which confirm the rule, at work luck alone is not sufficient. Or in any case:

Luck must be sought for methodically.

If, indeed, *those who start out well are already halfway to the end of their work*, after making a sound initial analysis, every choice and individual decision must be generated by a series of events which, however, are not always under the control of the manager or the people involved. These chains of events can determine the project's success or lack of success. They are external factors, macroeconomic developments, sudden competitive losses, events that have happened since the choices were made. In fact, every choice is made at a certain moment in time. And the alignment of conditions changes.

A leader has no need of a *Monday morning referee*. Who are the latter? The "Monday morning referees": the people who know everything because they watched the game the day after, ten times in a row, sprawled comfortably on the sofa at home, with 20 playbacks, 40 slow motions, and the commentary. "I told you so," they'll say. But only because they aren't *in* the game. In real life that's not how it is.

THE LEADER NEEDS PEOPLE TO HELP HER/HIM TAKE DECISIONS WHILE THE DECISIVE GAME IS BEING PLAYED

If we've taken the "right" decisions there, we'll try and repeat them, so as to make them into a virtuous cycle or *continuum* of decision-making. If instead the choices turn out to be wrong, the single passages will have to be analyzed with the necessary serenity so as to understand what went wrong or perhaps the mistakes that were made. In any case,

The important thing isn't not to make mistakes, so much as not repeat your mistakes obstinately.

To do this you mustn't become enamored (strictly) of your own ideas, visions, strategies. Leadership is

- a **DIRECTION** you want to follow;
- **STRATEGIC THINKING**;
- your own **INSTINCT**;
- accumulated **EXPERIENCE**.

The world changes: in basketball you play right up to the last second; every football game is a thing in itself; life is not made up of theories or schemes you can apply without considering the adversary; you don't get to choose the adversities. In any case, risk is implicit in any competition: there's inflation, the pandemic, or no pandemic. Briefly, what are the conditions you move in, and how do they change while we are stuck there, wherever "there" is? In this sense, it's important to modify your visions without distorting them, retaining the necessary solidity given by the original idea.

Doing | Michael Jordan
Alien

Air Jordan, when he jumped, stayed in the air for two seconds, 15 meters. He flew. It was 6 February 1988 when, at the NBA All-Star Game in Chicago, 18,000 people witnessed the slam dunk, which was very soon to become the most famous sporting move in the world: Michael Jordan was challenging Dominique Wilkins of the Atlanta Hawks.

Jordan is the Chicago Bulls' number "23": he sprints from the far side of the pitch, 28 meters of parquet, starts dribbling, and then leaps into the free line of fire, his flight covering 15 meters.

Fifteen meters of pure air.

At the height of his form, the vital statistics of the Bulls' shooting guard were 198 centimeters for 98 kilos, arm span of 210 cm, and his results were just as impressive: 32292 points, six times NBA champion, five times MVP of the Regular Season, and Defensive Player of the Year in the 1987– 1988 season, in 1999 voted "the greatest North-American athlete of the twentieth century", *last but not least* declared net assets of $1,310,000,000.

A life trajectory which is a perfect curve, a shot worth three points from the furthest corner of the field, an impossible position that starts with a kid from Brooklyn, the son of a bank employee and a mechanic.

As a kid, Michael was slightly built, to the extent of being excluded from the first local baseball team; the same thing happened when he tried to get into the Buckaneers basketball team: too short – the trainer chose another kid.

The year after, though, MJ grew – to a height of 190 cm. From then onwards *His Airness*'s career took off in the direction that has made him immortal (note: *The Last Dance*, the US sports docu-series created by Michael Tollin for ESPN and Netflix which was released in streaming in April 2020).

Capable of an inclusive leadership, geared to getting his fellow players to interact with perfect harmony and balance, integrating team spirit and talents, always fit and in the front line, Jordan has played under the worst of conditions – from food poisoning to the game after the tragic murder of his father – he embodies the empathetic leader, gifted with great emotional intelligence, capable of calling himself into question, learning from his own mistakes, and being a mirror and example for others (a similar lesson comes to mind from the attorney Atticus Finch, hero of Harper Lee's novel, *To Kill a Mockingbird*, played by Gregory Peck in the film of the same name of 1962).

"Once I took a decision, I never thought twice about it," says MJ in the docu-film telling the story of the myth and his deeds. Many uphill climbs and descents, difficulties and successes. It's a long road, but a true leader must be farsighted.

They mustn't be content with quick results; they must think **LONG TERM**.

A game can be won even at the last second, and if it's lost, failure is part of any career: we're human, says the alien, and if you tackle everything with passion, even when you lose, you'll have won anyway!

KEY TAKEAWAYS

"Our" leader

- uses the 80/20 rule and then, if needs be, "peels the onion!";
- knows that those who start out well, are halfway to the end of their work;
- has a **WE** culture (let's make a deal);
- wants to make things happen;
- decides today for today, within a vision that looks to tomorrow;
- doesn't persist in their errors.

CHAPTER 10
Vertical horizon

DOI: 10.4324/9781003378532-13

The leader must have a horizontal vision of the various different areas that make up a business unit, a company, their team, and must manage decisions on a horizontal plane. A person who, in the course of their career, has "climbed" to their present position, comes from one or two vertical competences they are specialized in: they cannot know everything. If they were to try and enter into every aspect of the business "vertically", it would prove impossible due to the time and the competences needed; this is why they will choose the best co-workers in each sector, so as to be able to delegate specific aspects of every situation.

ENTRUSTING THINGS TO ANOTHER PERSON, YOU MUST BE ABLE TO TRUST

The leader has a vision that is

- horizontal in terms of strategy;
- vertical in terms of sectors.

We might define this concept **VERTICAL HORIZON** (VH).

WHAT IS VH?

VH means having a vision, a horizon before you, having it in your head, in your inner world, knowing how to control the individual verticalities and being able to put them together, manage them, mix them, and take them apart, just like great artists or chefs or sports trainers.

In general the verticals are the following:

- the key components of each individual profession;
- a person's strong points;
- the skills an athlete has, just as in football there are different qualities that distinguish the great defender from the attacker or the great goalkeeper.

In a company the vertical components are as follows:

- product development;
- trading and sales;
- marketing and communication;
- administration and finance;
- management of the supply chain;
- operations;
- management control;
- IT systems and the digital world;
- development of human resources.

In professional life, instead, they are the experience gathered in the various different industries

or sectors in which the managers have worked, including the following:

- industrial manufacturing;
- fast-moving consumer goods;
- fashion, design, and luxury goods;
- services;
- transport;
- financial services and investments.

ALL THE BASIC ELEMENTS DEALT WITH IN THIS BOOK ARE INCLUDED IN VH

A book that has asked questions about the concept of leadership today and that can really be applied to every person who undertakes a journey, understood as research (in the dual metaphorical key of Musil, and of Jason and his Argonauts), therefore:

- the ability to **ATTRACT AND WORK WITH "GIANTS"** and other leaders, each with her/his own distinct character and their own *pluses* and *minuses*;
- the gift of **EMPATHY**;
- the sort of articulated **HUMANITY** that declines in many ways, including understanding work situations, your colleagues' or staff's problems;
- **KNOWING HOW TO BE** "personally" **CLOSE** to the individuals who are part of the company habitat.

THE **VH VISION IS CRISP, DETERMINED, COHERENT AND MUST BE CARRIED FORWARD IN THE LONG TERM, EVEN WHEN TRAVELLING THROUGH HOSTILE TERRITORY, WITH FALLS, OBSTACLES, DIFFICULTIES.**

In the uncertain river of time, VH is

- the strength of being able to be alone, at certain moments and for certain decisions;
- **THE CERTAINTY OF MAKING YOURSELF DISPENSABLE**: the true strength of every contemporary leader, chosen for the added value they can contribute to every situation;
- being able to enjoy popularity but also deal with unpopularity, thanks to being firmly "centered" on your own ideas, to the preparation achieved (if needs be, remember to always "list your own competences"), to a personality acquired through experience or natural talent reinforced by the right choices;
- having strong values engraved in your heart and in your mind, which then become the mentality and collective approach of the team;

- the confidence of "knowing how to do things" – or at least being able to give it a try;
- being able to accept fallibility, errors, without them prejudicing your self-esteem but on the contrary, so that they provide an impetus for coming objectives.

The leader, the manager, the person who can decline this multidimensional verticality, with the vision of a horizon, or a horizon of visions, is destined for great success.

In fact, if you have to manage a company, a family, and if you are in some way leader of it, you have to assume the responsibility, and therefore you must have a 360° horizon before you, giving an overview of all the necessary and useful elements. A leader certainly can't have specific competence in every field, but they must know how all the vertical components can lead to a general vision that brings them together and transforms them strategically into future achievements.

The *one-man band* leader of former times is an anachronism today, a contradiction. Today, the leader is the one who can see the horizon. And the one who gets help with the verticals from competent people. They are a talented manager.

THE LEADER IS THE ADDED VALUE IN THE COMPANY

A leader who works to become indispensable is not doing the company a service, as they spark off the concept of dependency in the company. Instead, they must do everything possible for the machine to be able to function perfectly without them. If they create machinery in which everything comes under their aegis, they will generate **DISCONTINUITY** (and this is extremely dangerous in the business world). If they are not present, on the other hand, things may not go as well as when they are, but they will nonetheless move forward (⇔).

The vertical horizon is a concept of vision based on competences.

Every horizon your eyes rest on, every vision or idea that surfaces will have under it as many pillars as it takes to support its weight. And below the pillars are the foundations: in this sense, then, **VH** is comparable to the Parthenon.

The important thing is not to become an arrogant leader but rather to be aware of "knowing you don't know", and this sort of leader will increasingly be a winner in the future. A leader builds up their **VERTICAL COMPETENCES** over the years. They grow, bearing in mind what the Americans refer to as humbleness, the humbleness of knowing that "you have to improve". This is why a leader builds a strong team around themselves – people they can work with and who can give an effective contribution to the company identity the specific leader has in mind. Seen in this light, the relationship with the leader is also a double act of trust and translation.

THE LEADER MUST BE ABLE TO USE STORYTELLING TO CONVEY THEIR IDEA

They must be able to make the journey attractive, be able to reveal the dangers but also the beauty of the adventure, which, however, remains their personal adventure until the crew embarks. Once the Argonauts have been identified, then and only then will it be possible to set sail for the destination. The goal, the objective of the enterprise. There will be difficulties, checkpoints will come along, losses, relative defeats, moments requiring complex management, and enemies to defeat. But there will also be co-workers without whom . . . nothing is possible. And then deals. And exciting projects. And objectives achieved. In the end it will be thanks to the vertical contributions from everyone that the horizon will be collectively attained – the horizon that is none other than the mark, **THE SITE-SPECIFIC VISION OF THE LEADER.**

The thought, the imaginary world that the leader carries within them finally becomes real (life, work, projects, products, business) – a tangible world: their own, that of the company, lastly OURS.

Join me and
we'll conquer
the world!

Vertical horizon | Bernard Arnault
Entrepreneur

Fashion, alcohol, hôtellerie, luxury yachts, *private*. Many brands and an extremely specific core competence revolving around a clear and equally remunerative thematic center.

In 2021, he is the second richest man in the world (after Amazon's Jeff Bezos) with assets estimated at 193.3 billion dollars. First and foremost, Bernard Arnault has great vision: all his choices revolve around the concept of "top of the line".

The son of an industrialist, right from the start Arnault knew he wanted to build the biggest group dealing in "luxury, beauty and goodness", briefly in the "well thing", and knew that to achieve this vision he needed the best in every sector: to get there, he first obtained excellent competences, graduating at the Paris École Polytechnique, then in 1971 entering the family business, and immediately afterwards the prestigious Dior brand.

His ability to attract the best makes him a sort of neo-Jason, and in fact he has created the LVMH Moët Hennessy Louis Vuitton SE brand, at present Europe's leading luxury group and the third most important worldwide, including brands like Dior, Bulgari, Fendi, Givenchy, Kenzo, hotel chains, L Catterton, Tag Heuer, Veuve Clicquot, Dom Pérignon, Tiffany, and Pinarello bicycles.

Horizon, vision, reliable people who are his delegates and act on his mandate, maximum efficiency in each individual competence, and a clear macro-objective – these are his strongest points. Over time, his staff has included top managers such as Tony Belloni, Pietro Beccari, Michael Burke, and Sidney Toledano.

Arnault is passionately keen on art and also a skilled pianist. In 2006, as a patron of the arts, he created the Louis Vuitton Foundation for creation and contemporary arts, an 11,700 sq m building-vessel hosting 11 galleries and situated in the Jardin d'Acclimatation, owned by the same LVMH group and which, by means of an agreement with the City of Paris, in 2065 will become public property.

All this goes to make up Bernard Arnault's vertical horizon, the conviction that only by taking on the best people in individual vertical competences will you reach your objective in a team. The complete, total horizon of your vision to contribute towards changing the world.

KEY TAKEAWAYS

"Our" leader

- has a horizontal vision of strategy and vertical competences;
- is the one who can see the horizon;
- is the added value of and inside the company;
- knows they don't know, has the *humbleness* that makes it possible to cultivate their own competences;
- is good at storytelling in conveying their own ideas;
- contributes to changing the world.

And now . . .
Make it happen

A SHORT BIBLIOGRAPHY OF REFERENCE WORKS

In writing this book, some of the texts listed below offered particular inspiration and food for thought.

Agassi A., *Open. La mia storia*, Einaudi, Torino 2015.

Burnison G., *The Leadership Journey: How to Master the Four Critical Areas of Being a Great Leader*, John Wiley & Sons, Hoboken 2016.

Cerni E., Zollo G., *Ulisse, parola di leader*, Marsilio, Venezia 2021.

Isaccson W., *Steve Jobs*, Mondadori, Milano 2011.

Lazenby R., *Michael Jordan. La vita*, 66thand2nd, Roma 2015.

Marquet L.D., *Leadership Is Language, the Hidden Power of What Your Say- and What You Don't*, Penguin Random House, New York City 2020.

Miller F., *300*, Mondadori Comics, Milano 2014.

Obama M., *Becoming. La mia storia*, Garzanti, Milano 2018.

Singh A., Mister M., *How to Lead Smart People, Leadership for Professionals*, Profile Books, London 2019.

Sun Tzu, *L'arte della guerra*, Feltrinelli, Milano 2013.

Welch J., *Winning*, Harper Business, New York 2015.

Whitman W., *Foglie d'erba*, Mondadori, Milano 2016.

Zatta D., *100 Strumenti per il manager*, Hoepli, Milano 2018.

Zatta D., et al., *Strategia e cultura d'impresa*, Il Sole 24 Ore, Milano 2008.

ABOUT THE AUTHORS

GIOVANNI BATTISTA VACCHI has been part of top management in public and private companies in Italy and abroad for over 25 years. As well as holding prestigious positions, including those of C-Level executive and CEO, he has taken on atypical roles in several industrial situations, ranging from luxury goods to real estate and transport, covering sectors from fashion to design. He has been CEO of Zucchi-Bassetti, Grandi Navi Veloci, and the American companies belonging to the Ferretti Group (Ferretti Group USA and Bertram Yachts); he has also acquired considerable experience in the private equity sector and in multinational strategic consultancy agencies, amongst which EY, The Carlyle Group, and Bain & Company. To his credit he has important experiences in international startups and other sectors and has dealt with growth and international development as well as company restructuring. At present he is CEO of the Colombini Group (Colombini Casa, Febal Casa, Rossana, Bontempi); he is on the Board of the companies Baldinini S.p.A. and Cantiere del Pardo S.p.A. (yachting industry). He teaches Durable Luxury Goods Management at the Università degli Studi di Bologna – Business School.

Giovanni Battista Vacchi graduated with honors in economy and commerce at the Università degli Studi in Bologna, later obtaining an MBA in Business Administration in the United States at Dartmouth College's prestigious Tuck School of Business.

If you would like to talk to Giovanni about any advisory work or speaking engagements, please contact him via email at: gvacchi@gmail.com

DANILO ZATTA is one of the world's leading advisors and thought leaders in the field of Pricing and TopLine Excellence. As a management consultant for more than 25 years, he advises and coaches many of the world's best-known organizations. The Financial Times defined him as 'one of the world's leading pricing minds'.

Dan has also been recognized amongst the *Top 5 Pricing Thought Leaders* on LinkedIn, in the list of the most engaging and impactful pricing thought leaders globally. The leading Italian business newspaper defined him as '*as one of the most recognized monetization authors in the world*'.

He has led hundreds of projects both at national and global level for multinationals, small and medium-sized companies as well as investment funds in numerous industries, generating substantial profit increases. His advisory work typically focuses on programs of excellence in pricing and sales, revenue growth, corporate strategies, topline transformations, and redesign of business and revenue models.

He is Head of Sales, Pricing & TopLine Strategies and Partner at the international management consulting company Valcon. Dan acted as CEO, Partner and Managing Director at some of the world's leading consulting firms, building up international subsidiaries, entire pricing and sales practices, and fostering growth.

Dan has also written 20 books including The 10 Rules of Highly Effective Pricing (Wiley, 2023), the international best seller The Pricing Model Revolution (Wiley, 2022), translated into 10 languages, At the Heart of Leadership (Routledge, 2023) and Revenue Management in Manufacturing (Springer, 2016). He has also published hundreds of articles in different languages and regularly acts as keynote speaker at conferences, events, associations, and at leading universities. He also supports as personal topline coach several CEOs of leading companies.

Dan graduated with honors in economics and commerce from Luiss in Rome and University College Dublin in Ireland. He got an MBA from INSEAD in Fontainebleau, France and Singapore. Finally, he completed a PhD in revenue management and pricing at the Technical University of Munich in Germany.

Connect with Dan on LinkedIn at linkedin.com/in/danilo-zatta

If you would like to talk to Dan about any advisory work or speaking engagements, please contact him via email at: zatta.danilo@gmail.com